A
PASSION
FOR
ANTIQUES

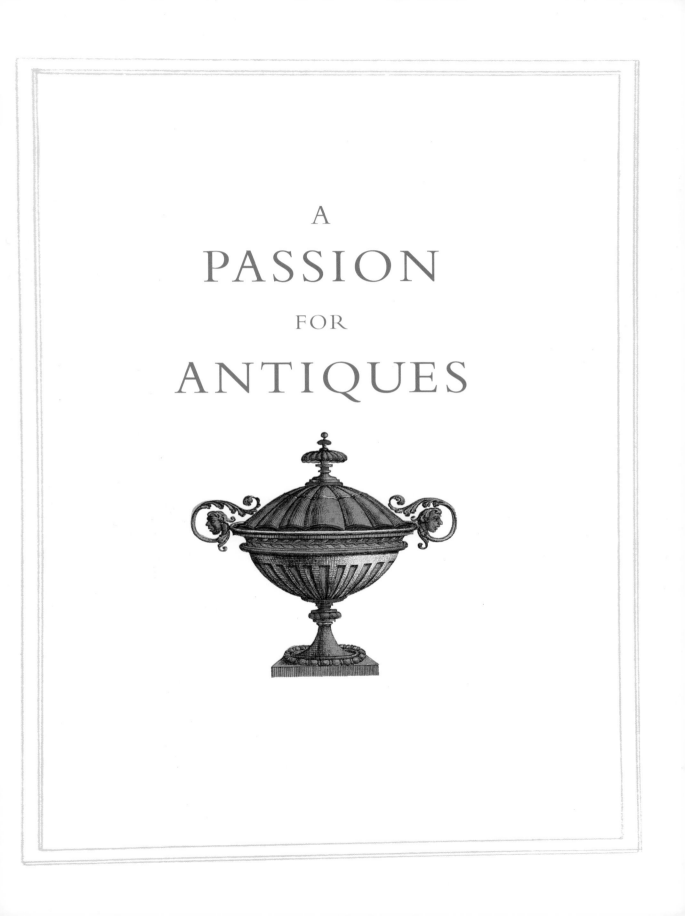

A PASSION FOR ANTIQUES

Barbara Milo Ohrbach

PHOTOGRAPHS BY JOHN M. HALL

Clarkson Potter/Publishers
New York

My first antiques book, *Antiques At Home,* began with this thought, which still seems so appropriate: *"To anyone who has rescued a neglected object and cherished it, tried to save a venerable building, or spent an afternoon sharing an older person's memories, to all who find warmth and lasting beauty in the old, this book is dedicated."*

for Mel

Published by Clarkson Potter/Publishers, New York, New York
Member of the Crown Publishing Group, a division of Random House, Inc.
www.crownpublishing.com
CLARKSON N. POTTER is a trademark and POTTER and colophon are registered trademarks of Random House, Inc.
Printed in China
Design by Jan Derevjanik
Library of Congress Cataloging-in-Publication Data
Ohrbach, Barbara Milo.
A passion for antiques / Barbara Milo Ohrbach ; photographs by John M. Hall.
Includes index.
1. Antiques.   2. Antiques in interior decoration.   I. Hall, John M.   II. Title.
NK1125.038   2004
745.1'075-dc22   2003024172
ISBN 0-609-60821-5
10 9 8 7 6 5 4 3 2 1
First Edition

Acknowledgments

All of us who have a love of old things share a common bond that inevitably brings us together. Traveling around the world to find the best of everything was a dream come true and encountering all the special people listed here, a wonderful dividend. It didn't matter whether I was in Helsinki, Rome, or New York City, there was always a connection because of our passion for antiques and collecting.

I am immensely grateful to everyone who helped me with this book in Ireland, a glorious country that is more and more extraordinary each time I visit. These charming people gracefully extended themselves and made our stay such an Irish delight: first and foremost, Ruth Moran and Damian O'Brien of Tourism Ireland and the Irish Tourist Board, whose invaluable assistance and planning made my trip such a success; Orla Carey of Tourism Ireland; the Merrion hotel, my Dublin home away from home, and charming Peter MacCann and Clare McNamara; The Knight of Glin, Desmond FitzGerald, and Madam Olda FitzGerald, and the kind hospitality of Glin Castle; Robert Duff; gracious Desmond and Penelope Guinness, Leixlip Castle; Kay and Fred Krehbiel; Stephen Mallaghan, Carton House Golf Club; Ruth Ferguson and Newman House; Dr. Muriel McCarthy and Marsh's Library; Joanna Cramsie and the Office of Public Works for the kind permission to include Castletown House; Geraldine Lynch for the kind permission to include Malahide Castle; the kind assistance of both the Fingal County Council and the Trustees of the Cobbe Family Collection and Brigid Dunne for permission to include Newbridge House; the Earl of Mount Charles, Slane Castle; George and Michelina Stacpoole; Ronan Teevan, Caxton Prints; Ian Lumley; Ian Haslam and William Maher, The Silver Shop; Chantal O'Sullivan, O'Sullivan Antiques; Gerard McDonnell; Geraldine Murtagh of Elegant Ireland.

The passion for antiques can take you to some very interesting places. I couldn't have done it without the great suggestions and assistance of Ally Flanigan and Lou Hammond; Victoria King; Alice Marshall; Sally Fischer; Gabriela Wolf, Eva Draxler, Sigrid Pichler, and the Austrian Tourist Office; Daniel Kennedy and Austrian Airlines; Riitta Frick and the Finnish Tourist Board; Maebeth Fenton Public Relations for Finland.

And in my other most favorite place, Venice, thank you to those listed here for their generosity and hospitality: Patrizia Serpe Piva; Francesca Bortolotto Possati and the staffs of Il Palazzo and the Bauer Hotels; Carla and Sergio Bortoli. Special thanks to Nancy Mernit Soriano and Monica Michael Willis of *Country Living* magazine and Jo Magrean for our adventures in Paris, and I'm much obliged to Karyn Millet, Jane Weldon, and Patti McCarthy, who had such good suggestions.

My sincere appreciation to all these avid collectors: Christopher Forbes and Margaret Kelly Trombly of Forbes; Michele Oka Doner and the Marlborough Gallery; Kathleen and Laura Doyle of Doyle New York; Jeff Lark, Grace Bibb, Doris Goddard, Pat Griffiths, and Bill Mihans of Sporting Collectibles at the Village Antiques Center; Antonia Salvato, Millbrook Antiques Mall; Ray Attanasio and Steve Abeles, Balsamo Antiques; John Anderson, Foxfire Ltd. Art and Antiques; Jim Cummings and Noah Fischel, Cummings Antiques; Timothy Dunleavy, Rural Residence; Jonathan Hallam, Hallam Antiques; Dee Keegan, Restorers of Fine Furniture and Interiors; Mark A. McDonald and the memory of Charles Millhaupt; Benjamin Wilson, Benjamin Wilson Antiques; Frank Gaglio, Barn Star Productions; Marni Bakst and William Sadler; Bonnie Tiburzi Caputo and Bruce Caputo; Betsy Ely; Michael Humphreys; Wanda and Greg Furman; Carole and Bill Castagnoli; Gail and Al Martin; Lee Ohrbach; Nicholas M. Pentecost; Eve Propp; Stephanie Stokes; Charlotte and John Suhler; Lisa and Peter Weidner; Stephen and Joanne Isola; and Kate Johns. I'm grateful to Lisa Newsom and Veranda Publications for permission to use several interior photographs.

Thank you to my literary agents and friends, Deborah Geltman and Gayle Benderoff, who have expertly seen me through twenty books; John Hall for his photography; Sallie Brady for her beautiful words; Barbara Tapp, Patti Verbanas, and all my associates at *Art & Antiques* magazine. And everyone at Clarkson Potter, especially my longtime editor, Annetta Hanna; Lauren Shakely; Marysarah Quinn; designer Jan Derevjanik; Natalie Kaire; and all the other dedicated people who always do such a terrific job making my books a reality.

Table of

Contents

ANTIQUING AROUND the WORLD

Herb. Millefolii

Introduction

As I sit down to write this, it's hard for me to believe that *Antiques At Home* was published fifteen years ago. I don't know about you, but I'm still avidly collecting. The thrill of discovering an unexpected treasure is as exciting for me now as it was years ago when I came across a Winsor and Newton fitted watercolor set on London's Portobello Road for my first collection, antique boxes. Though much has changed, it's still a great time to collect. All we antiques lovers have long known that age is beautiful and belongs in our modern lives. Of course, "age" is a relative term, with 1950s furniture and 1960s vintage clothing being snapped up today with the same fervor as eighteenth-century pieces that fulfill the criteria of being "real antiques," that is, more than one hundred years old.

The passion for the past, with which more and more of us seem to be smitten, is what encouraged me to pick up where I left off with *Antiques At Home.* I have heeded the requests of those who have asked for more about antiques in letters or by approaching me after my speeches at philanthropic events throughout the country. As a result, I've put together this second volume, *A Passion for Antiques,* which I hope will be not only useful in your antiques collecting but also enjoyable reading.

I still love reading the magazine *World of Interiors.* One reason is essayist Alistair McAlpine, who recently wrote in his column that "the world of art and collectors has changed beyond recognition in the last 50 years." It's amazing to consider that *Antiques Roadshow* had yet to air and the Internet barely existed when I last wrote about the world of antiques.

My life has changed, too. After almost twenty-five years, my husband, Mel, and I closed our antiques and home accessories shop, Cherchez. This allowed us the flexibility to indulge our other passion, travel, which has always gone hand in hand with our passion for antiques. *Art & Antiques* magazine enlisted me to trot the globe for them as Editor at Large, and other magazines, including *Departures* and *Southern Accents,* asked me to contribute to their pages. Recently, *Country Living*'s travel editor and I went to Paris, where we shopped the flea markets and my favorite antiques shops.

Over the years, it has given me enormous pleasure to share all the great things and sources I've discovered. Working on this book has been no exception because I've traveled to almost every important antiques lover's city, starting with my hometown, New York. It's been quite an adventure. As a result, in addition to being a design reference and primer on living with antiques, *A Passion for Antiques* is truly an antiques lover's Baedeker, filled to bursting with information and photographs of the many gorgeous homes and inspiring collections from around the world that I have been privileged to see.

Part I, "Pursuing the Passion," is a discussion of why we all collect, what motivates us to race out to antiques markets before the first light of dawn to engage in what some consider compulsive behavior, but we consider fun.

"Decorating with Antiques," Part II, is a decorator's dream. I was privileged to visit and photograph some of the most amazing homes and antiques for these chapters, and interview some delightful people, too!

PREVIOUS PAGE: *The tables in my house always end up displaying my favorite things—antique books, a nineteenth-century cast-iron urn, a brass Copia (the goddess of abundance), and porcelain plates overflowing with potpourri.*

ABOVE: *When it comes to blue-and-white china, I have one of everything, including teapots, sugar bowls, gravy boats, and cups big and small.*

BELOW: *My Winsor and Newton watercolor set in its wood box still has its original paints, brushes, and white porcelain dishes for mixing colors.*

For most of us, our collections are still works in progress. A famous London dealer says, "I just love to cheer up my nest with beautiful or useful things that sing to me, colors, textures, and forms that please and soothe, ravish and seduce." No matter how many doorways I step through, I am always intrigued by how people live with their antiques. On these pages you'll be sharing the delights I experienced when I entered these rooms.

Many of you know how important an appreciation of the past is to living well with antiques. "Essentials of Antiques," Part III, gets you started with four chapters on each of the major categories of antiques: ceramics, silver, glass, and textiles. Because most of us realize that we are merely caretakers for these precious objects, I include advice on how to preserve your antiques properly, with suggestions on care and storage in addition to lists of professionals to consult before undertaking any major restoration. You'll refer to these chapters again and again. Best of all, they can launch you into a community of fellow aficionados where you can join societies, subscribe to newsletters, and become a more informed expert on your subject.

Is there anything more stimulating and rejuvenating than travel? As an avid collector, I believe that travel is not just about shopping but also about educating our aesthetic palates. People who love antiques have a curiosity that overlaps into many other areas.

Part IV, "Antiquing Around the World," is a little book all on its own. It's filled with insider secrets and special out-of-the-way places I have discovered over the years. Included are favorite shops, the best antiques markets and what time to get there, auction galleries, unique small museums, and little-known historic homes that I love. And, in answer to so many of your requests, I've provided my tried-and-true list of outstanding hotels and restaurants. So if you have plans to pursue your antiques quest in any of the cities in this section, have fun.

It's almost a contradiction, wouldn't you say, that the passion for antiques is at an all-time high in an era of lightning-fast technological development? We aren't the only ones pausing to admire that fruitwood marquetry sideboard or the intricate stitching of an early American sampler. No computer program can duplicate these treasures or suggest the mysteries of their provenance: the person who made them and then the generations thereafter who used and appreciated them. It makes you feel lucky, doesn't it, to be able to live with these objects in your home today? That watercolor box that was part of my first collection still sits on a living room table. Every time I catch sight of it, it gives me a certain pleasure and, like so many things in my home, brings back fond memories of the past.

In *Antiques At Home,* I said that antiques are a curious pastime. Collections come in all shapes and sizes and so do collectors. What unites us is our common pursuit of a piece of the past, that particular object that excites our aesthetic and indulges our historical curiosities.

I can think of no better way of expressing that thought than by sharing the words of historian Harold Darling, who wrote in his charming book, *I Love Old Things,* "I love old things, ones that were made to last, and have lasted. I love them because they bring me closer to the past from which I grew, and to those who made and used them. I love them because I admire ingenuity, skill, and design, and because I feel that it is right to cherish that which has been cherished by those who came before me."

BARBARA MILO OHRBACH
NEW YORK

ABOVE: *On my last visit to Venice I unexpectedly hit the jackpot—a wonderful antiques fair in the nearby hilltown of Asolo in the Veneto. If you'd like to visit when you're in Italy, see page 174.*

BELOW: *I had to have these scrumptious 1920s French beaded flowers, colorfully displayed in the Puces de Vanves in Paris (see page 154 for more details). Who knows, they might end up on my favorite straw hat this summer.*

PURSUING

THE PASSION

the
QUEST

Ars longa, vita brevis
(Art is long, life is short).

The day I discovered that Sigmund Freud, the father of modern psychiatry, was a passionate antiques collector was a watershed moment. I had a fast flash of, Well, if he's okay, I'm okay. It was a confirmation of what I have always believed throughout all these years of treasure hunting and buying antiques: I have been doing something right all along, despite the exasperated sighs and raised eyebrows of family and friends who have put up with my endless antiques ventures.

PREVIOUS PAGE: *Rare mezzotints hang floor to ceiling in Dublin's coziest shop, Caxton Prints. A must-see for anyone pursuing the passion.*

LEFT: *You experience the human side of history when you stay in Ireland's Glin Castle, where family collections are on display, including an ancestral military uniform.*

In 1938, before World War II, Freud fled to London from Vienna, leaving behind some personal possessions, but transporting, at great cost, his library and his 2,300-piece collection of ancient Greek, Roman, and Egyptian antiquities, among other things. His housekeeper re-created Vienna in London, with every object in its proper place, and Freud continued to collect, feeding what he admitted was "an addiction, second only to nicotine." (If you want to see the collection, you can visit the Freud Museum in London; see page 164.)

A recent study in Great Britain and the United States revealed the fact that more than one in three of us collect. Why do we do so? The answers always intrigue me. Is it to rescue an imperiled object? To preserve a bit of history? A nod to nostalgia? For the thrill of the chase? For

15

investment purposes? To fill our lives with texture, richness, and beauty? The reasons are many and intersect and divide along the way.

As collectors we've been studied and compared to many things. A compulsive behavior expert at a Manhattan hospital found that a buyer's heart rate and blood pressure rise significantly and his brain releases feel-good serotonin when he finds a desirable object. The same physiological reactions/responses occur in a gambler who's placing a bet! Others have labeled us hunters, searching the wilds of one another's castoffs, stalking our prey with patience and perseverance. However, a recent article in the *New York Times* said that "new research contradicts the idea that collecting represents aberrant behavior. If almost half the population is doing it, you can't really call it peculiar!"

One of the joys (and, yes, addictive qualities) of collecting is that we can do it anywhere. I read recently of a Modernist architect whose quest for silver in the antiques markets of the world is a distraction from her day job, a treat to herself when she is traveling on business. I was reminded of my weekends scouring the Paris and London flea markets on breaks from my many business trips there scouting new fashion trends for *Vogue Patterns*. Those excursions brought me great pleasure—and, I'm happy to say, opened my eyes to much beauty.

It's been said that a true collector shipwrecked

ABOVE: *Chinoiserie panels and treasures in the Cobb family's c. 1790 "Museum of Curiosities" in Newbridge House in Dublin.*

BELOW: *Shell-seekers can even find their favorite motif in a frontispiece from a rare book.*

OPPOSITE, ABOVE: *A collection of handmade mother-of-pearl and shell snuff boxes with elegant silver and brass fittings.*

OPPOSITE, BELOW: *The weird and the wonderful: a close-up of Cobb family treasures from their world travels, including red wax seals and rare eggs.*

on a desert island would begin amassing seashells; or in a meadow, wildflowers. Scientists believe that we have a compulsive need to create a small world for ourselves with our objects, one that makes us feel safe and secure, one that we can control. I think Freud's story is testimony to that.

Aside from the joy of collecting antiques, I was reminded of the serious side of our pursuit and the great potential a collection may have when I read that the British Museum started as a private collection. Now 7 million items strong, it continues to grow. "Collecting," said the museum's director, Dr. Robert Anderson, "leads to an understanding of the past, categorization of knowledge, and sheer enjoyment."

I've learned never to underestimate the value of some of the objects we live with, especially today as the definition of "collectible" expands. With the advent of optimistic bidders on Internet auction sites, more people than ever are collecting. While it may seem more difficult now to find affordable pieces to add to our collections, the market *has* opened up, introducing new categories of antiques and collectibles that aren't always as old, but someday will be just as valuable—and treasured. What are some collectibles to watch out for? Dealers, collectors, and colleagues of mine offer these unexpected suggestions: military uniforms; 1950s furniture; 1960s barware, china, and silver from shuttered hotels and old cruise liners; antique cameras; handpainted miniatures;

OPPOSITE AND ABOVE: *Being a longtime shell collector, I've always wanted to see the ultimate. Created for the Countess of Kildare in 1760, Shell Cottage at Carton House is adorned with lustrous shells from around the world.*

BELOW: *If you garden, as I do, why not collect the vintage pieces you find along the way. Some gems: turn-of-the-century seed catalogs, handmade flowerpots, tools, and a garden club award from yesteryear.*

Disney memorabilia; early mezzotints; designer costume jewelry, accessories, and vintage clothing; antique garden implements; architect-designed furniture; space-exploration artifacts.

Trends aside, the experts still advise you to buy only what you love. Lady Victoria Leatham, the chatelaine of Burghley House, a stately home in England filled with extraordinary objects, said in a recent *Country Life* interview that some of the favorite pieces in her Asian ceramics collection were "bought cheaply in a Knightsbridge arcade selling decorative bits and bobs." Experiences like that keep us coming back.

Ready to go shopping, or overwhelmed? Don't be. Just remember this nice thought from Beverly Nichols, the English garden writer who himself collected passionately: "If you possess even one beautiful object it teaches you more, by its proximity, than a hundred visits to museums." So, let's go shopping!

BELOW: *An inlaid tallboy showcases bronze souvenirs from the Grand Tour: an ewer, a tazza, an urn, obelisks, and an incense burner.*

OPPOSITE: *When you collect something small and precious, such as these rare Irish portrait miniatures painted on ivory, you'll never run out of room.*

Kathleen and Laura Doyle

ADVENTURES AT AUCTION

I always look forward to visiting Doyle New York. I like to check in on its previews and see what goodies I can't live without. And I'm always happy to spend time with its chairman, Kathleen Doyle, and her twenty-five-year-old daughter, Laura, who heads the jewelry department in the gallery started by Kathleen's late husband, William Doyle.

Those of us who lived in New York City in the early 1960s remember Bill's first shop in midtown. In the summers, he held estate-sale auctions at the VFW Hall in East Hampton on Long Island. As my husband and I were just married and had a beach house there, they were something we looked forward to. Bill had a great eye for antiques to go along with his easygoing, charming manner. We still enjoy many of the treasures we bought there.

Kathy said that Bill always loved old things, and she told me this lovely story: "He went to his first auction with his aunt when he was a child. He desperately wanted a wooden box that several other people in the audience were interested in, too. There was a bidding war and finally everyone began chanting, 'Let the kid have it.' So for $4.25 he had bought his first antique."

In 1973 the successful shop moved to East 87th Street, where it still is today. It became William Doyle Auction Galleries, and when Bill Doyle died unexpectedly, his wife took over the business. It has grown by leaps and bounds to become one of the most well-respected auction galleries in the United States.

When asked about the current state of the auction market, Kathy and Laura finish each other's sentences. Their enjoyment of the antiques auction business and of each other is readily apparent.

Q. *How does Doyle New York differ from other auction galleries?*

A. Kathy: Our goal is to be user-friendly, and our experts are always available to answer any questions, be they large or small. We have tried very hard to make the auction process understandable and accessible to everyone, especially those who have never attended an auction before—the new buyer.

A. Laura: My mother really has focused on education with our lecture series and programs with local colleges here in New York City.

Q. *What does the gallery specialize in?*

A. Laura: Everything from fine-art paintings and elegant antique jewelry to vintage clothing and the decorative arts—for example, a perfect good-quality coffee table for a newlywed's apartment.

Q. *How do you find great merchandise?*

A. Kathy: Antiques are really a treasure hunt . . . you never know when you are going to discover the pot at the end of the rainbow. For example, in the Joan Payson Whitney auction that we held several years ago, one of the items was a rent table with lots of drawers. A dealer was examining the table thoroughly when two pieces of paper fell out—one was a document signed by Walt Whitman and the other was Abraham Lincoln's last public address! The table had been looked at by hundreds of people. The gallery has also auctioned

PREVIOUS PAGE: *The mother-and-daughter auctioning duo in their Upper East Side Doyle Galleries.*

off the wardrobes of many notables, including Bette Davis, Ruth Gordon, and Gloria Swanson.

Q. *What do you think people will be buying five years from now?*

A. Laura: There are always things that are overlooked. Certainly, as people become more aware of what has appreciated from the past, they are keeping more things from the present, such as *Star Wars* figures, toys, and items that may be related to pop culture, like lunch boxes.

Q. *What are the earmarks or characteristics of a good collector or collection?*

A. Kathy: Curiosity, developing an eye, and looking for objects that can be stars in building a collection. One should stay open to the market, be in the market and ready to buy at the right price and at the right time.

Q. *Is it still caveat emptor? What assurances does the buyer have that the provenance or description of an item purchased at auction is accurate?*

A. Kathy: The most important thing for a buyer to do is to read the catalog thoroughly. It will educate you. It lists, among other things, the conditions of sale and all the different guidelines, by categories, such as furniture and fine paintings. We offer seminars that people can attend so they can become better educated about the auction process. They are held once a month on Sunday mornings and cover all the helpful hints, including the steps for buying and selling at auction.

Q. *Has the Internet or eBay changed your business?*

A. Kathy: We were the first New York auction gallery to post our catalogs on the Internet free of charge. The website is fully interactive. You can click to the expert, just as if you were in the gallery, to ask questions about a piece you may be interested in. You can also leave bids with us online. Our website is open 24-7 so you can view the catalogs, check our auction schedules, and read our press releases from anywhere in the world. We have a "virtual personal shopper." For example, you can tell us what you collect and are looking for and we will e-mail you if the item is in one of our upcoming sales so you can bid on it.

Q. *Do you personally collect anything? Don't you get tempted working here?*

A. Laura: Both . . it's an occupational hazard. I collect Georg Jensen table silver. I just got married and I told my fiancé that I come fully furnished!

A. Kathy: Laura has a wonderful eye and buys whatever is stylish at a price. I collect French furniture and vintage costume jewelry and things for my children, who are now settling down and starting to collect.

Q. *What are some reasons for buying at auction?*

A. Kathy: There are several good reasons: generally more variety and choice, all in one place; one does not have to make a commitment—it's less intimidating to just wander; if you know something about an object that no one else has picked up, there is always the chance for a real bargain; if you grow tired of something you bought at auction, you can in turn auction it in the future.

My Tips for Buying Online

Millions of items of interest to collectors are offered on the Internet every day. For me, this will never replace the challenge of an auction or the thrill of searching in a corner of an antiques shop, blowing away the dust, and finding an unexpected treasure. Yet sales have grown by leaps and bounds as people discover that the antique they've always dreamt of can sometimes be found much more easily from their computer keyboards at home.

You must be a savvy consumer when buying on the Internet, as the landscape is constantly changing. The buyer must beware. Here are several commonsense tips to help you avoid potential problems:

- Always use a credit card, if possible, so that you have some recourse if you are not satisfied with your purchase or if it has been misrepresented. If you don't want to send your credit card details via e-mail, you can always telephone the seller.

- For further protection, especially when making a large purchase, consider an online escrow account with a company set up for this purpose. This prevents the seller from receiving payment until you are satisfied with the merchandise. You are usually charged a percentage of the purchase price for this service.

- Be sure to discuss commissions, shipping costs, and insurance costs prior to completing your transaction.

- Look for authenticity guarantees and be sure you have the option to return an item if it is not as described or as pictured. On the most reliable sites, the seller has been vetted, there is a guarantee of authenticity, and you are assured a level of security.

- If you're just starting out, pick up *Kovels' Bid, Buy, and Sell Online,* published by Three Rivers Press, for more in-depth information.

—BMO

DECORATING

SUMMER
BED ROOM

DUCHESS.S
SittingRoom

WITH ANTIQUES

After many years of visiting fellow antiques collectors in their homes and photographing their treasures, I am still endlessly intrigued by the different ways we live with our antiques. From the restraint of a Minimalist who might feature one perfect Shaker table in a spare city apartment, to the Romantic who layers a Victorian farmhouse with vintage linens, shelves of old baskets, and Sprig china, we create countless moods with our beloved collections, mini self-portraits that express our personalities. "Magic is born of mixtures," said Madeleine Castaing, last century's doyenne of French design. Indeed, half the fun of collecting is the mixology that goes on at home, creating interesting combinations of masterpieces and oddities, bargains and splurges.

PREVIOUS PAGE: *Upstairs, downstairs . . . When you ordered your breakfast tray in the eighteenth century, a bell like this rang in the servants' quarters.*

OPPOSITE: *A room with a view—and a Gothic window flanked by French armchairs.*

I'm always inspired by the lifestyles of the people I photograph for my books, whether a tastemaker in a Venetian palazzo or a dedicated conservationist living in a castle in Ireland. I find myself slipping them into different collecting categories like the Romantic, the Individualist, the Minimalist, the Connoisseur, and the Free Spirit, which fill the following chapters. I'm a bit of a "nosy Parker" at heart and have an endless curiosity about how people develop a passion for particular things and decorate their homes with them. In the chapters to come you'll meet some of my favorite antiques lovers and see how they live with their treasures. I hope you'll pick up some wonderful ideas along the way, as I did.

Mario Praz, the Italian connoisseur who wrote the classic book *An Illustrated History of Interior Decoration,* said that he had an instinctive mistrust of anyone who wasn't interested in objects. I agree. When it comes to living with antiques, my personal philosophy is to enjoy and appreciate every moment of the journey—and the arrival.

the
ROMANTIC

*She could scarcely see an object
in that room which had not an
interesting remembrance connected
with it.*

—JANE AUSTEN,
Mansfield Park

As I read that quotation, I'm doing

a visual tour of my own sitting room,

lingering over each treasured antique and conjuring up a remem-

brance. Family heirlooms share space with unexpected discoveries

from my travels and pieces of furniture I fell for like a star-crossed

lover. "I don't want anything new," Christian Dior said when

decorating his home. "It has to have a well-worn feel to it, old and

rich in memories."

The Romantic is an emotional collector, which is not to say that she doesn't buy intelligently. But for the Romantic an antique's provenance is as much about its history, the lives it touched, as it is about its value. A Romantic might start reading up on English silver because of a lonely pair of Victorian candlesticks inherited from a relative, or collecting Lalique glass because of a wedding gift.

I recently read about a woman whose family has lived in the same house for a century—with the accumulation to prove it. She says that her treasures—the jumble of antiques and the

PREVIOUS PAGE, LEFT: *A full-blown pink poppy handpainted on porcelain by Worcester, c. 1810.*

PREVIOUS PAGE, RIGHT: *Nineteenth-century romance: A graphic Dufour wallpaper panel is the perfect foil for the salmon toile de Jouy quilt atop a sleigh bed at Leixslip Castle.*

OPPOSITE: *In Glin Castle—a wonderful way to celebrate a collection of Worcester plates that normally would be stacked in a cupboard.*

ABOVE: *Mixing and matching your china (especially blue-and-white) is much more interesting than using all the same pattern.*

MIDDLE AND BELOW: *A close-up of a woodland scene on a lady's penwork dressing table, with a silver clothes brush, a papier-mâché pintray, and the unexpected—lemons in a pierced-porcelain compote.*

chipped cups that her aunt always bought because she felt sorry for them—show "an understanding that history is made up of minutiae, as well as great events." A reassuring thought the next time you need to justify splurging on that Art Nouveau lamp or an early silkwork sampler hand-stitched by a young schoolgirl many years ago.

Mrs. Henry (Sister) Parish, who layered rag rugs and quilts with old painted furniture "rescued" from inns in Maine, understood the romantic warmth of decorating with antiques, a philosophy she shared with many clients. Her colleague Albert Hadley, who continues her decorating legacy, likes to hold up a bunch of flowers and say, "Look, none of these match, but they all go together." This describes the home of many a Romantic.

"It's not the houses I love, it's the life I live in them," said Coco Chanel. And the life of a Romantic is one of nostalgic elegance, as exemplified by the dramatic interiors of romantic Leixlip Castle, the home of the Honorable Desmond Guinness.

Am I a Romantic? When it comes to collecting, I'm a little bit of everything, but I guess that anyone who can't write a book without quoting Jane Austen answers that question.

OPPOSITE, ABOVE AND BELOW: *Putti frolic in the brilliant Pompeian-style frescoes at Castletown, Ireland's finest Palladian country house—a must-see for anyone who loves classical architecture and decoration. Marble statues fill each niche in the Long Gallery created in the 1770s.*

ABOVE, LEFT: *Flowers and country scenes in Staffordshire and Willow-pattern gravy strainers and plaques look wonderful on a bright-yellow wall.*

ABOVE, RIGHT, AND LEFT: *When the wallpaper that the eighteenth-century lady of the house ordered from China for the boudoir ran short, she resourcefully cut panels from the paper and decoupaged them onto these dramatic peacock blue walls. Standing in the middle of this magical room is quite an experience, amplified by the aging silvered mirrors in gold-leaf baroque frames.*

PREVIOUS PAGE, LEFT: *Only a romantic would leave this chair in all its worn grandeur.*

PREVIOUS PAGE, RIGHT: *The patina of old leather adds romance to this rare nineteenth-century Irish sofa, which rests under a wall of antique mezzotints.*

OPPOSITE: *The color of springtime provides the perfect backdrop for handpainted Chinese watercolors on rice paper and a gilded ormolu clock by LeRoy & Fils, Paris, on the fireplace.*

LEFT: *Inset mirrors in a door reflect the serenely elegant room within.*

BELOW, RIGHT: *A bust of William Pitt set on an ornate gilt pier table circa 1830.*

BELOW, LEFT: *Vintage silver reticules in a guest bath —a clever way to display your treasures.*

OVERLEAF: *The amazing c. 1765 Print Room at Castletown. Housebound aristocratic ladies cut-and-pasted engravings to the walls on rainy Irish days.*

Desmond Guinness

A FASCINATING CONSERVATIONIST

The Honorable Desmond Guinness has dedicated most of his life to saving countless endangered buildings that would otherwise have been lost. In the 1950s and '60s few people in Ireland were interested in Irish furniture or pictures, and the demolition of important historic architectural gems was commonplace. It was then that Desmond Guinness was stirred to action. He and like-minded friends founded the Irish Georgian Society, an organization that has done so very much to preserve art and architecture in Ireland.

His lecture brochure modestly states that he is a conservationist, a historian, and a noted speaker. That description is just the tip of the iceberg. His mother was one of the famous Mitford sisters and he is a charming, beguiling, and accomplished man of many parts. He has written six books, including the elegant and definitive *Great Irish Houses and Castles, Dublin— A Grand Tour,* and my personal favorite, *Palladio.*

As if this wasn't enough, in the 1960s he financed the purchase of the threatened Castletown House, thereby saving what is now acknowledged to be one of the most significant Palladian country estates in the world.

Castletown is what led me to Desmond Guinness in the first place. For years, I had been clipping articles on this unique place. But even so, I was unprepared for its breathtaking beauty. Begun in 1722 in the style of a sixteenth-century Italian palace, its interiors reflect the charming taste and sensibility of Lady Louisa Connolly, one of the stylish Lennox sisters who in

1758 supervised its redecoration. (We were lucky to be able to photograph its neoclassic Pompeian wall paintings and the famous Print Room on these pages.)

I met with Desmond Guinness in his comfortable library at Leixlip Castle in County Kildare. Built in 1172, it's a romantic house that stands at the meeting of two rivers, the Rye and the Liffey, just ten miles from Dublin. It is furnished with family treasures and the extraordinary eighteenth-century Irish furniture, paintings, architectural drawings, and objects that he and his late wife, Mariga, started collecting when they were first married. In the classic book *The Inspiration of the Past,* the noted historian John Cornforth said of them: "They didn't have much money to spend on its repair or furnishing. . . . They were in those days seeking out good furniture that was cheap, because it had had a hard life and, what was then considered unusual, leaving it unrestored."

The impression of Leixlip Castle is one of an elegant country house that manages to be unfussy at the same time. For many years it was the nerve center of the Irish Georgian Society and has always welcomed anyone interested in Irish art and culture. In Sybil Connolly's book *In an Irish House,* Desmond Guinness says, "We like to welcome people interested in Irish art and culture to Leixlip. Museum groups from the United States are quite frequent visitors; these are often subjected to a slide talk on Irish architecture given by myself in the drawing room. Sometimes new members for the Irish Georgian Society are gained in this way (sometimes, no doubt, they are lost!)."

PREVIOUS PAGE: *The Honorable Desmond Guinness in his sitting room in front of a life-size wooden doll-house. The inside is completely furnished.*

ABOVE: *Another view of the sitting room gracefully adorned with lovely objects, a result of a lifetime of discriminating collecting.*

Q. *Did you always collect? Did you collect anything as a child?*

A. When I was twelve years old, I bought a bronze clock with a glass dome that I thought was just too wonderful. My mother said, "Darling, please don't let it leave the bedroom." I still have it and now I think it's ghastly.

Q. *When did you start collecting Irish antiques?*

A. In the 1950s, especially after we purchased Leixlip Castle in 1958.

Q. *What did you collect? What was your most memorable purchase?*

A. Eighteenth-century Irish pictures, furniture, and Delft pottery. It seemed appropriate to furnish Leixlip with Irish things as far as possible, although the carpets are French. And what a moment it was to hunt the salesrooms! Country houses were selling up left and right, and large pieces were going for a song. Standing at the back of a dispersal sale in Mr. Naylor's antiques shop in Dublin I heard a nine-foot table going for just a pound, and bought it because we needed a kitchen table. It turned out to be a blackened mahogany Irish side table with grotesque masks and a marble top, which has been much published since in articles on Irish Georgian furniture.

Q. *Where do you buy now, strictly through auctions or would we ever bump into you in a Kildare boot sale?*

A. Today I buy mainly in shops in order to find the right thing for the right place. Dublin's best is Johnston Antiques on Francis Street.

Q. *As a historian, an author, and a conservationist, how did you educate yourself about your field of interest?*

A. It was during my three years at Oxford University, and I grew up at Biddesden in Wiltshire.

Q. *Why did you start the Irish Georgian Society?*

A. When we moved to Ireland, we became aware of the destruction of beautiful buildings in Dublin, which was progressing at a rapid pace. I began to sound people out and in 1958 we revived the original Georgian Society into the Irish Georgian Society. There were sixteen original members and we dedicated the society to art and architecture in Ireland with particular emphasis on the years 1700 to 1830. It is now forty-five years old and has thousands of members throughout the world.

Q. *What does the Irish Georgian Society do today? Can anyone join?*

A. The society focuses on the conservation and protection of Irish buildings of architectural merit. We're involved in fund-raising, education, and making grants. Yes, anyone can join and participate in our events program of lectures and tours. They also will receive our journal and be able to visit select historic houses in Ireland at no cost. We have branches in many cities of the United States. [The details on how to join are on pages 145 and 170.]

Q. *People are always curious as to how you became involved with Castletown.*

A. The Connolly family, amazingly, continued to live at Castletown until 1965, when the house was sold. In 1967 I was able to acquire the empty house with one hundred acres. Most of its contents had been sold at auction and dispersed. It was in terrible condition, but a tremendous amount of work was done by volunteers to put it right and subsequently we opened it to the public. In 1979 I gave the house to the Castletown Foundation so that it could be further preserved. Later, the house was transferred to state care and is now managed by Dúchas, the Heritage Service of Ireland, which has undertaken a major program of restoration. It is one of the most important houses in Ireland and significant in terms of European architectural heritage.

the
INDIVIDUALIST

I believe in plenty of optimism
and white paint.
—ELSIE DE WOLFE

There's no defining Individualists. They're like the fabulous cook who never consults a recipe and the impeccably dressed friend who always looks of-the-moment in what inevitably turns out to be a twenty-year-old Yves Saint Laurent. They possess that intangible, genetically coded, have-it-or-don't-have-it quality: taste. You know the home of a great tastemaker when you walk into it: the surprising juxtapositions of old and new, the self-assurance of mixing furniture and objects from different periods and styles, of

PREVIOUS PAGE, LEFT: *Glass matchstrikers in shades of rose reflected on a silver salver.*

PREVIOUS PAGE, RIGHT: *A French Empire sleigh bed updated with a bazaar's worth of Turkish pillows.*

ABOVE: *Rare Russian icons make a powerful picture when assembled together in an unlikely spot.*

RIGHT: *A collection of "poor man's silver"—mercury glass candlesticks and globes beautifully reflect light.*

OPPOSITE, ABOVE: *Too much is never enough for a lover of cranberry glass.*

OPPOSITE, BELOW: *Old parchment sketches of glassware from Venice's Salviati glass factory become art.*

combining high and low, and the effortless way that it all comes together.

Some of history's great Individualists we remember not only for the antiques they collected but for the way that they lived with them. Tastemaker extraordinaire Madame de Pompadour is credited with creating what we think of as eighteenth-century French style. Her influence was far-ranging and she filled her châteaux and Louis XV's palaces to bursting with elegant objects and furniture. Nancy Mitford wrote in her biography of Madame de Pompadour that she "excelled at an art which the majority of human beings thoroughly despise because it is unprofitable and ephemeral: the art of living."

Mario Praz, Pauline de Rothschild, and Nancy Lancaster are all on my list of forever-inspirational Individualists. Many of them, I know, took their lessons from Parisian antiques dealer and interior designer Madeleine Castaing, who was still running her legendary shop on the rue Jacob well into her nineties. Castaing earned the sobriquet "queen of the flea markets." During the war, she bicycled through occupied Paris at 4 A.M. to pick through the flea markets. Talk about a role

model! She filled warehouses throughout the City of Light with Biedermeier furniture, Belle Epoque treasures, and anything that she loved. Her credo? "One should avoid boring things."

Cecil Beaton remembers legendary connoisseur Charles de Beistegui's terrace overlooking the Champs-Élysées, a "hodgepodge of Napoléon, Le Corbusier modernism, and Louis Quinze furniture that had been painted white and placed on a grass carpet." A frightening yet intriguing picture!

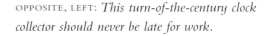

OPPOSITE, LEFT: *This turn-of-the-century clock collector should never be late for work.*

OPPOSITE, RIGHT: *An assortment of flea market coronation biscuit and chocolate tins in the "tartan room."*

OPPOSITE, BELOW: *Precious keepsakes on my Fortuny-covered dressing table, including a seventeenth-century embroidered purse and a silver fig from Buccellati.*

LEFT: *Native American beaded souvenir bags in sundry shapes from the 1800s form a unique backdrop for old picture frames.*

BELOW, LEFT: *Lacquered painted wood Guantiera trays with typical Venetian motifs.*

BELOW, RIGHT: *A colorful assortment of beaded Victorian reticules nestled in a bowl on a tabletop.*

The lesson here is that Individualists collect neither the trend of the moment nor what the latest auction gallery says is a good investment, but what they love. The results can be surprising. That's precisely why it's hard to say exactly *what* it is that Individualists collect. Renaissance objects, eighteenth-century French porcelains, architectural elements, Art Deco designs, African tribal carvings, you name it— so maybe there's hope for us all. In fact, in this chapter, single-minded Christopher Forbes of the publishing and collecting Forbes family tells me how he became a collector by specializing in the memorabilia of just one man— Napoléon III.

ABOVE: *There was a time when a tin toy collector was considered an Individualist—not anymore. European and American tin toys from the 1880s.*

MIDDLE: *Painted cast-iron canine door porters are charmingly decorative as well as functional.*

BELOW: *Appealing lithographed phonograph record needle tins fit perfectly in the triangular-shaped drawers of this screw-and-nail chest.*

OPPOSITE: *A classic Wooton desk, with all its nooks and crannies, is the ideal place for a friend to display her collection of cigarette and tobacco tins from the 1890s to 1940s.*

Chairs are as individual as people. Some are simple, others complex. Some welcome with comforting arms and others cause discomfort. Henry David Thoreau once said, "I had three chairs in my house; one for solitude, two for friendship, three for society."

TOP ROW, LEFT TO RIGHT: *Someone handpainted these green country chairs in a very unique manner.*
This well-endowed armchair—now ready for a second life—was sitting in an antiques shop in Helsinki, Finland. A gold-stenciled American kitchen set with a well-painted apple.
This loving-hands-at-home was sold in the first ten minutes of a summer antiques show.

MIDDLE ROW, LEFT TO RIGHT: *The dealer didn't know,but my guess is that these beauties are 1920s French.*
A self-satisfied, overstuffed Victorian needlework chair with an intricately woven sewing basket of the same period.
A delicate, yet very dignified Windsor, burnished with years of wear.
This 1940s fabric-covered armchair is displayed with typical French chic at the Marché aux Puces—note the deep purple suede gloves.

BOTTOM ROW, LEFT TO RIGHT: *A set of gold Italian chairs sits on the market cobblestones of Asolo, Italy. Blowsy flowers are needlepointed at random over the back and seat of this very comfortable-looking chair. Lacquered nineteenth-century papier-mâché with tufted velvet seats.*
Someone handmade this country chair with curved twigs and painted it a lovely color.

Christopher Forbes

THE CONTRARIAN COLLECTOR

Christopher (Kip) Forbes is a charming collector who is happy to share his knowledge in a wonderfully accessible way. He has a passion for collecting, is a tireless champion of the Victorian Society, and as vice chairman of Forbes and overseer of the collections for the Forbes Galleries is responsible for a treasure trove of objects enthusiastically collected by his father, Malcolm Forbes.

The items included the world's largest collection of Fabergé eggs and objects; more than five hundred toy boats made from 1870 to 1950; American historical documents; ten thousand toy soldiers; and trophy memorabilia.

The Forbes Galleries, on lower Fifth Avenue, is open to the public. A favorite insider secret to many, it's a special place that reflects the soul of a collector who enjoyed every moment of the hunt and is the perfect place to bring children or that budding collector in your family.

Kip Forbes's stylish Manhattan office above the galleries is remarkable on two counts. First is its stunning decor, which includes one of his favorite pieces, a richly colored 1855 portrait of Empress Eugénie (Napoléon III's wife) and her court. It is a magnificent floor-to-ceiling, wall-to-wall copy of Franz Xaver Winterhalter's famous oil painting and dominates the entire office. Second, although the office was humming and the desk piled high with papers, there isn't a computer or any electronic equipment in sight. Only a telephone. A kindred spirit!

Q. *When did you start to collect?*

A. When I was seven or eight years old, I started collecting comic books, which I loved. I still collect *The Flash*. Then, when I was at Princeton, around the time I was doing my senior thesis, I started putting together a collection of Victorian paintings, which spurred my interest in Napoléon III.

Q. *Was your father an inspiration?*

A. Oh yes! The five of us siblings are following in his collecting footsteps. It is through him that we inherited "the disease." My father got it from his mother, who, although she didn't collect much, loved to shop. My dad was an inspired collector and a great mentor. Once when we were on the *Highlander* docked at Saint-Tropez, he and I went foraging for antiques. My father kindly bought me the first piece of my collection, an official portrait of Napoléon III by Hippolyte Flandrin. It was something I dearly wanted, so it was my Christmas and birthday present that year.

Q. *Is that when you became interested in Napoléon III?*

A. Like most Americans I wasn't aware that there was more than one Napoléon. But I'm a contrarian collector. Napoléon I was not affordable and his nephew Napoléon III was eminently affordable and still is. As I became more enthusiastic about Napoléon III, I started collecting. He was emperor of France from 1852 to 1870 and responsible for good things like the reconstruction of Paris under Baron Haussmann. And yet his inconsistent leadership style made him a contradictory politician. Like many Frenchmen, he was on the side of the South during the Civil War, so he's not a favorite of some people in this country. On the other hand, he was defeated in the Franco-Prussian War and so the French are still not fond of him. An interesting person to collect.

Q. *What kind of Napoléon III objects do you collect?*

A. Staffordshire figures, paintings, bronzes, plaster busts, coins, glass, china, folk art caricatures, letters, and memorabilia having to do with him and the time in which he lived.

Q. *What makes you buy something?*

A. As long as it's connected in some way with Napoléon III, I'm interested. I believe that all collectors need their fix on a regular basis, whether they can afford it or not. It's that acquisitive instinct, whether it's Hummel figures or green stamps—we all want to collect something. If you are a true collector, no matter what your means, there's always something to collect.

Q. *Where do you find the most pieces?*

A. Obviously the big supply is in France, but some of my best finds have been bought in other places. For example, I just acquired Napoléon III's surrender letter from the Franco-Prussian War of 1870 at a London auction. I recently discovered a new dealer at the Marché aux Puces who sells only royal and imperial souvenirs. He has been appallingly helpful and keeps finding lots of wonderful things for me to buy! If you can find a dealer who knows your taste and what you're looking for, he can be a great help in adding to your collection.

Q. *Do you have any tips for new collectors?*

A. My key was to find a niche, something that not too many people were collecting. Find something that interests you—which you love—and stick with it because you will keep finding interesting

additions. For example, an office associate whose last name is Phoenix collects vintage glass by the same name. There are so many options now with eBay and the Internet, that it makes collecting accessible to all.

Q. *Are you still buying at the same pace? After all, it's been over thirty years.*

A. Oh yes! There's just one disappointment, though. With the switch to euros, I can't delude myself anymore. It was easy before. I could be very vague. Now I know exactly what I'm spending!

PREVIOUS PAGE: *Christopher Forbes in his delightfully decorated office sitting in front of a dramatic floor-to-ceiling painting of Empress Eugénie.*

ABOVE, LEFT: *Staffordshire figurines from Forbes's collection of Napoléon III objects.*

ABOVE, RIGHT: *Don't be surprised if you bump into Forbes at the Marché aux Puces looking for more distinguished portraits.*

the MINIMALIST

Less is more.
—MIES VAN DER ROHE

Mies van der Rohe's philosophy might seem anathema to anyone who has fallen under the spell of antiques. But Minimalists love their treasures, too—they just have fewer of them. The quest for perfectionism drives this collector, a preference for one rare piece of Chinese export porcelain over a breakfront heaving with lesser quality; one perfect Bauhaus chair over a room full of secondary pieces; several place settings of burnished Continental silver over a drawerful of contemporary Gorham.

PREVIOUS PAGE, LEFT: *A Turtleback desk lamp of green Favrile glass on a double-front Mission desk by Gustav Stickley.*

PREVIOUS PAGE, RIGHT: *A celebration of simplicity: a Frank Lloyd Wright table designed in 1939 for a Wisconsin home; a set of c. 1910 Prairie School black chairs; a Gustav Stickley sideboard. The leaded-glass-and-bronze Arts and Crafts chandelier is also from the same period.*

LEFT: *A silverplate water jug c.1854 by J. A. Stimpson sits atop an old-fashioned radiator.*

ABOVE: *This country kitchen seems Minimalist until you open the cupboard doors, which hide a secret passion for white American Ironstone pottery of all shapes and sizes.*

I think there's a reason why today we see an increasing number of super-selective collectors. It's because the affordable supply of antiques that existed only thirty years ago simply is not there. Undaunted, "objet" lovers who lack the resources of the Rockefellers or the Gettys have learned to make choices, exercise self-restraint, and employ a decorating style that celebrates each and every one of their purchases.

Although we might assume Minimalists are drawn particularly to all things Moderne, that's not always true. They might be as likely to collect

American folk art or Scandinavian Gustavian furniture as they would be to own the early designs of Finland's Alvar Aalto and Russel Wright ceramic dinnerware.

Pauline de Rothschild, who had a budget anyone would envy, said that if there's nothing fine enough to fill a space, one should leave it bare. But socialite Eugenia Huici Errazuriz, who also kept a Parisian apartment full of well-edited art and antiques, takes that a step further. "Elegance is elimination," she said. Then again, she did go on to become a lay Franciscan nun—and, of course,

ordered her habit from Chanel! A most elegant way to eliminate worldly things.

I've been collecting since I was a teenager and have always loved "stuff." I love the objects, the buying, the research. Having had my shop, Cherchez, for more than twenty years, I developed a collecting lifestyle. But now, the airy uncluttered life of the Minimalist seems very appealing to me. I never thought I'd say this, but I'd love to have less to fuss with, worry about—and clean.

So perhaps I should take my own advice for antiques lovers who want to live more like Minimalists. Do as the designer Karl Lagerfeld did and send some of your treasures off to auction, giving others a chance to enjoy them. Or you can rent storage space and put part of your collection there to be dealt with at a future time. It may be easier not to go cold turkey. Consider packing up some of your objects for a seasonal or biannual "rotation." When you unwrap that tissue paper months later, you'll feel the heady rush of discovery all over again. If, on the other hand, either of these ideas appeals to you primarily as an opportunity to fill up your newly emptied spaces, then forget it, you'll never be a Minimalist.

OPPOSITE: *An interior designer's clever solution: Display multiples in same-sized frames for a clean, uncluttered look.*

ABOVE: *Back to nature: A small collection of birdcages decorates this whimsical country escape.*

BELOW: *These fashion drawings (now a hot collecting category) were tucked away in a file until the artist's daughter discovered these 1940s treasures.*

OPPOSITE: *Objects and furniture created by contemporary designers and architects are destined to be the antiques of tomorrow. Here a Frank Gehry Easy Edges chair, designed for Knoll in 1971, and a ceramic multicolored vase sculpture designed by Ettore Sottsass dominate a loft space.*

ABOVE: *A set of 1939 Frank Lloyd Wright upholstered wood chairs, originally designed for Sondern House in Kansas City, now in a private home, atop a French Art Deco carpet.*

LEFT: *Contemporary beauties in a relaxed setting: an Isamu Noguchi–designed 1954 wire pedestal table, Charles Eames classic chairs from 1945, and an orange Anywhere table lamp from Greta von Nasseny, 1952.*

the CONNOISSEUR

I find I like fine old rooms that have been occupied in a fine old way.
—HENRY JAMES

There's much to be learned from the Connoisseur—about eye, education, and, dare I say, self-restraint. The Connoisseur is a true collector, not an accumulator, one who would be satisfied returning from a European buying expedition with one tasteful antique rather than an ocean-liner container full of lesser objects. When I think of connoisseurship, I always harken back to the Grand Tour, that rite of passage for well-born seventeenth-century Englishmen (and later Americans), who would spend years touring the

Continent, soaking up the paintings and sculptures of classical Italy; the antiquities of Greece; and the appointments of *les grandes maisons* of Versailles. Some of them became famous collectors: the Earl of Arundel, John Tradescant, Horace Wadpole, and Sir John Soane, to name a few. The purpose of the Grand Tour was to absorb culture and cultivate taste. Isn't that why we travel today?

Modern-day connoisseurs continue to be inspired by the classical, collecting old master paintings, marble busts, mosaics, architectural renderings,

PREVIOUS PAGE, LEFT: *A fine Venetian decoupaged and lacquered eighteenth-century workbox in pristine condition.*

PREVIOUS PAGE, RIGHT: *Good taste permeates every corner of Francesca Bartolotto Possati's study, from the embossed books to the* cartonnier *behind the brocade desk chair.*

OPPOSITE: *The front hall in Glin Castle boasts eighteenth-century Irish side tables, a Fortuny-covered wingchair, and a former lady of the house, Nesta FitzGerald, painted while on her honeymoon in Rome in 1882.*

BELOW: *Sunlight streams in from the Grand Canal into a* piano noble *that is pure Venice: handpainted frescoes, eighteenth-century blackamoors, and ormolu sconces.*

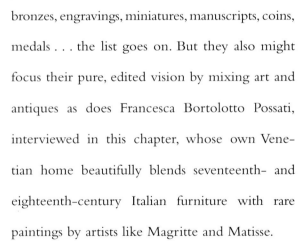

bronzes, engravings, miniatures, manuscripts, coins, medals . . . the list goes on. But they also might focus their pure, edited vision by mixing art and antiques as does Francesca Bortolotto Possati, interviewed in this chapter, whose own Venetian home beautifully blends seventeenth- and eighteenth-century Italian furniture with rare paintings by artists like Magritte and Matisse.

I'm afraid my mail carrier has suffered greatly over the years under my efforts at connoisseurship. Every new area of antiques collecting can bring with it a plethora of reference books, specialty

ABOVE, LEFT: *Chinese and Staffordshire figurines under a c. 1810 Boston gilt mirror in yellow paint.*

ABOVE, RIGHT: *An early Chinese faience statue blends beautifully with Italian antiques from the eighteenth century.*

OPPOSITE, CLOCKWISE FROM LEFT: *Only the best will do for connoisseurs. A Chinese mahogany Chippendale shelf displaying rare Meissen and Chinese figures and brilliant Chinese porcelain parrots. Breathtaking 1765 rococo plasterwork by architect Robert West at Dublin's Newman House. A heart-stopping Dutch rosewood trumeau topped with blue-and-white Delft and Chinese porcelains. An eclectic collection of wood and ivory desk accessories and serendipitous finds.*

OPPOSITE: *Living in Manhattan with priceless antiques (and the ever-present laptop).*

RIGHT: *This collector has hundreds of pieces of blue-and-white Peony pattern by Wedgwood. An Italian painting is reflected in the mirror.*

BELOW: *Classic architecturally themed souvenirs from the Grand Tour, including miniature models in plaster and alabaster, paintings, and a building fragment, are displayed under a nineteenth-century portrait of a hunting dog.*

magazines, auction catalogs, and memberships to organizations. In the end, though, I'm a more knowledgeable collector.

When it comes to buying, knowledge often leads to an unexpected find. Recently, in the bottom of a tattered cardboard carton, I spotted a cache of black-and-white engravings of urns printed in London in 1777 that I snapped up for a song. Collecting like a Connoisseur doesn't have to be expensive.

It's also the way that Connoisseurs live with their treasures that I admire. Interior designer Lady Henrietta Spencer-Churchill, who grew up surrounded by treasures in Blenheim Palace in Oxfordshire, was right when she said, "antiques should be treated like paintings, as works of art, and displayed sympathetically and to their best advantage."

CLOCKWISE FROM ABOVE: *Oil landscapes and antique porcelain pieces from around the world.*
A fascinating assemblage of objets de vertu, *including silver vinaigrettes, tortoise and silver pique snuff boxes, filigree patch boxes, and even a silver whistle (upper right).*
Bronzes, family pictures, and a gallery glass at home on a tabletop.

OPPOSITE, CLOCKWISE FROM ABOVE LEFT: *I love the way the Venetian light reflects in this mirrored plateau in the center of the dining table. At night, the Murano glass chandelier does the same.*
A sophisticated combination: orange Chinese glass jars, an Austrian clock, and a contemporary Italian bowl on an eighteenth-century pier table.
This vision greets guests on their way to breakfast at Glin Castle. The majestic front hall, filled with family portraits and treasured pieces of Irish furniture, will put any antiquarian in a wonderful mood even before coffee.

ABOVE: *The distinctive sitting room of Venetian connoisseur Francesca Bortolotto Possati features a dazzling collection of Venetian paintings and a rare painted corner settee from the magnificent palazzo Ca' Rezzonico, now a grand museum.*

OPPOSITE: *This glorious vision greeted me when I arrived to interview collector Possati in her home on the Grand Canal; an eighteenth-century museum-quality sideboard with original paint depicting Chinese scenes topped with a spray of centuries-old Venetian beaded flowers.*

And, in the end, isn't that the hallmark of a true Connoisseur? They wouldn't think of not honoring their antiques with perfect placement, because, after all, these objects are, and will continue to be, part of their everyday lives.

Francesca Bortolotto Possati

FIVE-STAR COLLECTOR

I spent a month in Venice when I was working on this book, which is where I met antiques collector and hotelier Francesca Bortolotto Possati. We had tea on the inviting terrace of Il Palazzo, her fabulous new boutique hotel on the Grand Canal. She is an energetic woman with impeccable style and a broad knowledge of antique European furniture and paintings, which is reflected in all aspects of her life.

As a child, Francesca Bortolotto Possati was really the Italian version of Eloise—instead of the Plaza, her second home was the Bauer Hotel, which was owned by her grandfather, who had purchased it in the 1930s. In 1997 she inherited the hotel, becoming its president and CEO, and also opened the exclusive Il Palazzo in an elegant eighteenth-century palace attached to it. By combining her entrepreneurial savvy, honed while living in the United States, with her passion for antiques, she has created comfortably opulent surroundings for her guests.

The lobby of Il Palazzo, shimmering with reflections of the water outside, is decorated with eighteenth-century Venetian lacquered panels painted with Chinese motifs—it's like being in a magnificent jewel box. Francesca's taste—quintessentially Venetian with a dash of chic elegance—is evident in each room. Luscious Rubelli and Bevilacqua silk cover walls and windows, while beds are finely carved by descendants of the original artisans. Delicate handblown glass chandeliers from Murano cast a romantic glow over everything. The renovation has seamlessly combined state-of-the-art technology with the traditional craftsmanship for which Venice is so well known.

Francesca passionately loves her city and all its irreplaceable treasures and is a board member of Save Venice, the international organization that has done so much to restore so many of its endangered buildings and objects. (The details on how to join are on page 175.)

Q. *When did you realize you loved antiques?*

A. I've been surrounded by antiques since birth. My first crib was a magnificent piece made by Andrea Brustolon, the superb eighteenth-century Venetian furniture carver. It seems I was aware of the importance of the crib even then, because as a child I was always attracted to beautiful things.

Q. *What did you first collect and why?*

A. I did not have a particular preference except perhaps for boxes. I've always liked any kind of shape in materials such as wood, marble, glass, decoupage, lacquer, textiles, et cetera.

Q. *Was anyone in your family an inspiration?*

A. My father had a great passion for decorating and was very knowledgeable about antiques, especially furniture. My grandfather collected in a different way. For a long time, he bought what no one else wanted. He was way ahead of the market and that turned out to be a very smart thing.

Q. *What is your philosophy of decorating with antiques?*

A. Pure aesthetic pleasure!

PREVIOUS PAGE: Collector Francesca Bortolotto Possati in her beautiful home.

ABOVE: Behind every connoisseur is a vast store of knowledge. In her library, Possati's stacks of book threaten to overwhelm a very generous coffee table.

Q. *What makes you buy something? Color, design, age, rarity?*

A. There are many reasons, but visual impact is the first thing I consider when purchasing objects and works of art. I am fascinated by color and very interested in the history and age of the object.

Q. *Which are your favorite galleries or antiques shops in the world?*

A. Apolloni in Rome; Silva in Milan; Wildenstein in New York; Peretti in London; Didier Aaron and Seguera in Paris.

Q. *Some favorites in Venice?*

A. Pietro Scarpa and V. Trois.

Q. *You have so many wonderful books. Which are your favorites among them?*

A. I love all my books. They are so numerous, but I remember and treasure every one. Like most book lovers, I can't stop buying them and I am constantly forced to find new shelf space. Occasionally, they are placed on hold in the attic until we can find more space. Oddly enough, if I need to locate a special volume, I somehow know exactly where to find it! Art books have an important place in my heart, together with some old French poetry books.

Q. *Do you have any tips for collectors?*

A. Always follow your instincts and educate yourself by finding out as much as you can about the source or the artist of every piece you like.

Q. *If there was an emergency and you could take only one antique with you, what would it be?*

A. As it would be impossible to carry heavy furniture, large paintings, or books, I would try to take my jewelry and two small paintings—one by Guardi and the other by Matisse and, if possible, a small early Venetian glass basket.

Q. *What's your best antique or vintage find?*

A. A precious gilded wood panel of the Madonna and Child from Tuscany. It was found in Siena hidden in a wall covered by plaster.

Q. *Do you feel you are safeguarding all these treasures for future generations? Has your love of antiques rubbed off on your children?*

A. Absolutely. Both my children are so attached to every single object and painting that they would be very upset if I attempted to change anything. Since they were very small I have exposed them to art and collecting. I often buy paintings for them as birthday presents. They love it and their taste and sensitivity to art and antiques impresses me.

Q. *How did you approach designing the rooms at your Hotel Il Palazzo at the Bauer in order to create an eighteenth-century ambience for guests who require twenty-first-century accommodations?*

A. I have lived in an eighteenth-century palazzo all my life, so this was easy. I also lived and worked in the United States for ten years. The combination of the two different experiences resulted in the perfect final result. I planned the design of the hotel as if it were my own home. In a private house, every guest room is different from the other. Even though people may be unaccustomed to living with antiques, I am sure that the moment they walk into a room they will feel the difference and enjoy it.

Q. *As a board member of the important organization Save Venice, what do you think the future holds for your beautiful city?*

A. I see a great future for my city. The love, respect, and care that so many people around the world are paying to this beautiful place makes me very optimistic. In the future I would like to see science and technology utilized together to safeguard Venice and enable it to face the future and maintain its standing as the only city in the world where the delicate balance of beauty, art, and a magical atmosphere mix together as nowhere else.

the
FREE SPIRIT

*If you fall in love with something,
that's all that matters. Your love
protects you from all upsets.*
—BILLY BALDWIN

We all know at least one of these
exuberant antiques collectors.
They can't abandon you fast
enough at the entrance to the flea market, taking off on their own
in search of the Holy Grail. They return hours later, all smiles, with
colorful cigarette and tobacco tins, nostalgic Christmas decorations
from the 1950s, old comic books or magazines, fishing paraphernalia,
or Mickey Mouse ephemera—brand-new additions to their quirky
collections.

Free Spirits are impulsive collectors who buy from the heart. Their antiquing is fun, a genuine extension of their personalities. Over the years, I've learned hard lessons from them. While many of us were still lolling over high-priced Americana and French Country, they were out there snapping up Biedermeier that now commands impressive hammer prices at auction; rag rugs that have found their ways into museum collections; and vintage couture for which many a Hollywood starlet might trade her Golden Globe. Their eccentricity has unexpectedly paid off.

The whimsical trailblazing of clever, ahead-of-the-curve Free Spirits should be watched (especially when you're next to them at a flea market

PREVIOUS PAGE, LEFT: *You don't have to be a Free Spirit to appreciate the durable and vivid color of today's highly collectible Fiestaware, which comes in so many wonderful, and useful, shapes.*

PREVIOUS PAGE, RIGHT: *Color and shape delight this collector, who aptly positions a classic 1956-design Marshmallow sofa by George Nelson under an exciting woven optical fantasy by Victor Vasarely.*

OPPOSITE: *Booties, sandals, Mary Janes, oxfords, slippers, boots, moccasins—who in the world ever thought there were so many red shoes? This collector travels the world, picking up children's shoes from the 1840s to the 1930s and never returning home without a find.*

BELOW: *This young-at-heart collector's father built narrow Lucite shelves, which fill all four walls of a special room devoted to her collection of 1950s and '60s wind-up toys. Mickey stands guard!*

and they fix their eyes on something fabulous!).

When Lady Dorothy Nevill, an early Victorian, began fancying Georgian furniture and Sèvres teacups, it was thought quaint and unusual. As the years passed and she saw English "cottage life" slowly becoming extinct, she began rescuing ordinary things like kitchen utensils, farm tools, and iron-work. "Old rubbish," she recalled her peers calling her eccentric collection, but she later reveled with "complete vindication" when her "rubbish" ended up in London's Victoria & Albert Museum.

Some Free Spirits, like former *New Yorker* editor Robert Gottlieb, who collects vintage ladies' handbags, and Rod Stewart, who rocks out for toy electric trains, have object fixations, while others, like a friend who has a collection of red children's shoes, go wild for color.

"What an intense life the colors have," painter Pierre Bonnard wrote to Henri Matisse. Indeed, color can be so intoxicating. Think of all that charmingly mismatched china, the wonderful painted rustic wood furniture perfect for country and beach houses, the rainbows of 1950s Venetian glass, Clarice Cliff's Bizarre ware, and jubilant 1970s fabrics from Marimekko.

You can become a Free Spirit, too, by

OPPOSITE, LEFT: *The colors in a vintage World War II poster coordinate with those in this cupboard of assorted Fiestaware.*

OPPOSITE, RIGHT: *Very collectible—and lovable— stuffed dogs guard a stack of vintage leather luggage.*

ABOVE: *Turn-of-the-century miniature lead figures, called Nuremberg flats, on Victorian platform mirrors create a vintage Christmas display on an Ohio quilt. All are hot categories for collecting right now.*

LEFT: *A jewelry collector's niche: Gold, pearl, and ivory brooches with a handpainted eye were tokens of love in the eighteenth century.*

OVERLEAF, LEFT: *In this Irish kitchen an old apothecary, with labels for each herb, sits under an eclectic collection and a sign that offers sound advice.*

OVERLEAF, RIGHT: *This collector—a commercial airline pilot—loves all things aeronautical and uses her vintage model collection as dinner party centerpieces.*

following the advice of Alistair McAlpine, who suggests collecting "something that is intensely personal, something that appeals to you regardless of what others feel about it, appeals to you regardless of price or material value." That's just what artist and collector Michele Oka Doner has done.

LEFT, ABOVE AND BELOW: *Free-spirited collector Michele Oka Doner appreciates the aesthetic of her books, especially the Egyptian volumes in her library.*

BELOW: *Found objects: Ancient Egyptian hieroglyphics on a tombstone, seals, scarabs, shells, and a meteorite.*

OPPOSITE: *Juxtaposing antiques with art, Doner positions a Victorian papier-mâché chair in front of a sculpture-laden piano.*

Michele Oka Doner

A COLLECTOR'S EYE

Inside the white, open loft created by the particular eye of sculptor, furniture designer, and collector Michele Oka Doner, the hustle and bustle of New York City seems to disappear. Her home and studio in downtown SoHo—she moved in during the 1970s before it was the thing to do—is what one would imagine an ideal artist's surroundings to be, a visual delight of old and found objects.

I first admired Doner's work when I was living in Florida, where she started out, and I have been following her career ever since. She has received much publicity for her intricately designed half-mile-long walkway in the Miami International Airport, which features two thousand buffed bronze elements from the sea embedded in a floor composed of dark terrazzo and mother-of-pearl. It's like walking through the surf at the beach.

Private collectors around the world have created a growing demand for her furniture pieces—designs that are lyrical and strong at the same time. Graceful chairs, tables, and screens are worked in textured metals like bronze, silver, and gold. They are stunning works of art and surprisingly comfortable furniture all at the same time. "Metal is my chosen medium," Doner says. "It is primal. You take ores from the earth and mix them to exactly the right strength . . . you are the sorcerer's assistant."

Doner's studio reflects her very personal style and sophisticated taste.

Groupings of objects are juxtaposed with precious antiques, all comfortable together on surfaces throughout the apartment, including atop her desk and even her piano. Found objects of all sorts are everywhere—shells, rocks, metal foundry scraps, fragments of vegetation, remnants gathered from the world around her, especially Miami, which she calls home. Enormous dried palm fronds lean against walls salvaged from the beach, where she finds much inspiration. All combine with her interesting collections of antique pieces —rare, old books; ancient Columbian sculptures; intricate Japanese silver; and Egyptian artifacts. A collector's spirit imbues every nook and cranny.

Q. *Where are you from?*

A. Miami—I had an agrarian childhood. Miami was the last place where I could grow up the way I did. I always loved working with my hands. I picked up what fell on the ground and manipulated it. Then I studied at the University of Michigan and that is where I started to do my work.

Q. *When did you start collecting?*

A. I started collecting as a child. I had a shell collection because we would go to Sanibel Island. I also started a butterfly collection, which I treasured.

Q. *What do you use for reference?*

A. My references are animal, vegetable, and mineral. A project takes me from one thing to the next in a very exciting way. I'm now working on something that features winged things, so I've been studying birds, moths, and bees, which have then taken me to Greek mythology and Icarus. The bees have brought me to hexagons and from there into animal architecture. One thing natu-

rally segues into another. I'm never bored. I feel that each piece is a journey, an exploration. My work is a tone poem; it keeps flowing and it's musical.

Q. *Why do you collect what you do?*

A. All of the things I collect go back to my love of shape, form, and texture. My pre-Columbian pieces, Egyptian scarabs, Chinese Buddhas, and Peruvian sculptures all reflect this natural organic feeling. I like mixing unexpected objects together—a precious antique piece next to beautifully formed natural things like rocks or shells.

Q. *You have an incredible collection of books. Why?*

A. I love collecting books. The old books are so beautiful with their embossed bindings. The Egyptian ones are the core of my library. They date from about 1850 to 1920. I was always interested in Egypt. As a child I was intrigued by the letters *gypt* of Egypt. Where else have you ever seen these letters in that order? Then one thing led to another and now it's floor-to-ceiling books. I accumulate books wherever I go and I have an abiding love for them.

PREVIOUS PAGE: *Michele Oka Doner in front of her cast bronze sculpture* Skrim.

OPPOSITE, ABOVE: *Turn-of-the-century parchment, pewter, copper, and wood Bugatti side chairs flank an eighteenth-century pier table topped with Peruvian, Asian, and natural ephemera.*

OPPOSITE, BELOW: *More rare Bugatti, here a settee and an armchair that Doner showcases alongside her own splendidly original work, a cast-bronze table called* A Radiant Disc.

ESSENTIALS

OF ANTIQUES

Every time an object catches my eye, whether it's in a Maine antiques shop or at New York's Winter Antiques Show, as an inveterate collector, I start to wonder: What is the history of this object? How old is it? Who made it? Is it valuable? Is it a reproduction? What is its condition? How can I clean it? Where will I put it? How will I store it? (The last two are sometimes the hardest questions of all!)

After decades of antiquing, I can usually answer most of those questions for myself. So that you will be able to do the same, in this section I've included lots of information on the most popular categories of antiques as well as personal tips on how to care for your treasures.

I've divided this section according to material—the way many people collect antiques. So, you'll find here chapters on ceramics, silver, glass, and textiles, each chock-full of essential information on history, care, and cleaning and a mini reference library of sources for further reading, lists of replacement and matching services, and just about everything else to get you started or to help you continue your antiques adventures.

The English historian Sir Kenneth Clark said he started buying antiques because of "a sentimental feeling that I must rescue them from neglect." I often feel that way, too. In the end, we're not merely owners of these objects, but their custodians, responsible for seeing that they make it to the next generation in the best possible condition. This can sometimes be a challenge, but it's part of your obligation as a collector.

If you're ever daunted, think of the Duchess of Devonshire, who rose to the occasion when her husband inherited the magnificent 175-room Chatsworth. She said, "I used to think you could arrange one of the big rooms upstairs, and that it could be frozen like a photograph, and that nothing need be changed as long as it was kept clean. I was wrong. Curtains, bed hangings, coverings on furniture, bindings must be fed, paintings on walls and ceilings restored, carpets mended if old and beautiful . . . it is like running to stand still."

Indeed, but isn't it worth it?

PREVIOUS PAGE: *One-stop shopping at a Dublin antiques shop on Francis Street.*

OPPOSITE: *Handsome books do furnish a room.*

CERAMICS

I once came across an amusing
quote from Oscar Wilde in which
he said that it was difficult for him
to live up to his collection of blue-and-white china! Such is the beauty
of ceramics. From the number of you who have written to me about
your own blue-and-white china collections after seeing mine, I'm sure
you'll appreciate that Wildean thought.

Exquisitely decorative, delightfully functional, and alluringly historical, ceramics are among the most satisfying antiques to own, but
they can also be among the most encyclopedic and confusing to collect. Without getting too technical, here are some basics. As always, I

recommend that you educate yourself—consult books, surf the Web, visit museums and antiques shops and you'll be ready when an incredible find is literally within reach.

Remember this: Terra-cotta, majolica, and bone china are all different but all ceramics, just as hydrangeas, snapdragons, and roses are all flowers. Ever since Neolithic times, when clay was shaped and air-dried back in 10,000 B.C., we've been blessed with centuries of objects. Think of all of those urns and vases that we know so well from the Metropolitan Museum of Art and the British Museum that were created by the Egyptians, Greeks, Etruscans, Romans, and, the true master ceramicists, the early Chinese. Most of us aren't fortunate enough to collect such exquisite, costly masterpieces, but contentedly focus on the European, later Chinese, and American ceramics that followed.

Let's start with the difference between pottery and porcelain. In the beginning there was pottery, made of baked clay and distinguished by its dense, opaque appearance—hold it up to light and the rays do not pass through. Pottery comes in a rainbow of colors depending on the mineral quality of its clay. It can be left unglazed (think of bisque or terra-cotta) or glazed (when metallic oxides like copper, iron, and manganese produce a variety of deep hues) and fashioned into everything from English Whieldon stoneware figures to Chinese tomb figures. Italy's majolica, France's

PREVIOUS PAGE, LEFT: *European subjects provide graceful decoration for delicate Chinese export porcelain pieces.*

PREVIOUS PAGE, RIGHT: *Isn't your mouth watering looking at this endless pine sideboard filled with one of everything you'd need in a country kitchen?*

BELOW: *A pretty collection of creamware.*

Quimper, England's creamware, and America's Rockingham (sometimes known as Bennington ware) are all examples of pottery.

Porcelain originated in China (hence the name china), where potters mixed kaolin, a pure white clay that all porcelain is made of, with a local feldspar, or rock mineral, to create a durable, translucent, finer-quality ceramic. The Chinese excelled at the production of this hard-paste porcelain, often called "true porcelain," which is distinguished by its smooth, glasslike glaze.

Enchanted with Chinese export pieces, Europeans struggled to duplicate them. First, they coated white earthenware with a tin glaze, creating Delft, or "poor man's porcelain." Later, they added ground glass to clay and a creamy, delicate, fragile soft-paste porcelain was born. Most eighteenth-century English porcelains and early Sèvres pieces were soft paste, and today are extremely rare and highly collectible.

But it wouldn't be long before Europeans developed hard-paste porcelains of their own. Johann Friedrich Böttger, an eighteenth-century ceramicist in Meissen, Germany, was the first to crack the code, and nineteenth-century England's Josiah Spode would add bone ash to clay and invent bone china. Thanks to all these geniuses we have the pleasure of savoring the visual feast of porcelains from France's Sèvres, Saint-Cloud, Chantilly, Mennecy, and Limoges; England's Chelsea, Minton, Coalport, Derby, Worcester, and Bristol; and Italy's Nove, Doccia, and Capodimonte. Not to mention, of course, Germany's Meissen, Ireland's Belleek, America's Lenox, and the centuries of treasures from the extensive reign of the Qing dynasty (1644-1911), when China's export ware was running full tilt.

As I said earlier, a buyer of pottery and porcelain is best equipped with knowledge, as well as a skeptical eye. Start by looking at the quality of painting and the modeling of the piece and consider when it was produced, as certain periods of a factory's production are more valuable than others.

Then examine the condition of the piece. Look for imperfections, hairline cracks, stains, or signs of repair or restoration. If it looks too new, be wary. More and more excellent-quality fakes and reproduction pieces are in the marketplace. Look at the bottom of a piece, which should have normal wear from years of being picked up and set down. Some plates may have minor cutting marks from knives. Run your finger over a piece to detect minuscule chips or cracks. If it's porcelain, try "pinging" it with your finger. You won't hear a noise if there is a hairline crack you can't see. It might sound like an extreme measure, but some collectors even carry portable ultraviolet lights to spot any sign of repair instantly.

Now turn over the piece to examine its mark. A mark may indicate the manufacturer or maker and can help approximate its age. Books on marks make fascinating reading for collectors (see "Suggested Reading" on the next page) and can help pinpoint the exact date and origin of a treasure.

Ceramic marks were generally applied four different ways: incised into the soft clay with a sharp tool; impressed into the clay by a stamp, resulting in a flat, mechanical appearance; painted on at the time of decoration with the name or initials of the maker; or printed with engraved copper plates.

While marks are an aid, they shouldn't be a decision maker. Many beautiful pieces have rubbed-off marks, no marks, inconsistent marks, or, sadly, fake marks. In 1891 the United States required that all imported pottery bear the country of origin. If "England" is there, you'll know the piece was probably made after 1890. In 1914 the law was amended to include the words "Made in" as part of the mark. "Made in England" is a clue that the piece dates from the twentieth century.

While every antique ceramics collector wants a collection of the finest quality, there will come a time when you'll fall for an object (maybe rare, maybe not) that's not in premium condition. With so many colors, shapes, patterns, and delightful purposes, it's hard not to be a little self-indulgent when you're a lover of ceramics. Just remember that condition is integral to the piece's—and your collection's—value.

SUGGESTED READING

Battie, David, ed. Sotheby's Concise Encyclopedia of Porcelain. *London: Conran Octopus, 1990.*

Chaffers, William. Collectors Handbook of Marks and Monograms on Pottery and Porcelain. *Los Angeles: Border, 1989.*

Godden, Geoffrey A. New Handbook of British Pottery and Porcelain Marks. *London: Barrie & Jenkins, 1999.*

Sandon, John. Collecting Porcelain. *London: Conran Octopus, 2002.*

BELOW: *A very special Rockingham dinner service with gold lions as knobs includes a meat platter and a large covered tureen.*

BELOW: *I have so many plates that I finally started making my own felt liners. The money saved goes toward buying more plates!*

If you love and collect old pieces of ceramics, you can appreciate the miracle of their survival from one generation to the next. Here are some suggestions that I hope will help you care for your collection.

Cleaning

Ceramics are fragile and must be handled with care, so don't rush when cleaning and washing them.

- Never put antique ceramics in a dishwasher.
- Use several layers of paper towels or a bath towel to cover the kitchen counter or work space when you're cleaning ceramics. That way, if something slips out of your hands, it will be less likely to break or chip.
- When washing an object, line the sink with towels or use a separate plastic bowl. Fill with lukewarm water and a mild detergent like Ivory dishwashing liquid. Water that is too hot or too cold could damage the piece. Rinse thoroughly before drying to prevent slippery surfaces.
- If the object has protruding pieces, such as delicate leaves or flower petals, use a cotton swab to clean those areas.
- Some pieces are too delicate to risk washing. Use a damp cotton ball or cotton swab to clean the object gently or a soft dusting brush or watercolor paintbrush for dusting.
- Restored, repaired, or unglazed pottery pieces should never be submerged in water for any length of time. Clean carefully using a cotton ball or a cotton swab.
- Dry the object carefully by hand or air-dry it in a secure place.

Storing

To prevent breakage, store your ceramics carefully.

- Do not put too many objects on one shelf and make sure the pieces are not touching.
- Store large objects in the back and smaller ones in front so you can see everything.
- Don't be tempted to put one ceramic piece inside of another. If you're like me, you won't remember it's there when you go to use it.
- It's okay to stack plates as long as you put something between them to prevent scratching. Quilted liners are sold in housewares stores for this purpose, or make your own felt circles and use them for years.
- When handling ceramics, never carry more than one piece at a time. Always lift from the bottom with two hands in order to support the object adequately. Do not lift by the handles, rims, or lids—no shortcuts.

Supplies

dusting brushes

ARCHIVAL SUPPLIES
800-628-1912
Fax: 800-532-9281
www.archivalsuppliers.com

felt fabric

JO-ANN FABRICS
888-739-4120
Fax: 330-463-6670
www.joann.com

felt liners

GRACIOUS HOME
1220 Third Avenue
New York, NY 10021
212-517-6300
Fax: 212-988-8990
www.gracioushome.com

Restorers

In case of damage to your treasure, you'll want to find the right professional to correct the problem. Without exception, all repairs and restorations on your valuable antiques should be done by experts. If you try to fix it yourself, you may cause irreparable damage or create more work for the restorer. A professional repair may be costly; only you can decide if it is worth it. Here are some tips:

- Your piece is precious, so make sure you employ a qualified person or company with a good reputation. Ask for recommendations from previous clients.

- Whenever possible get at least two estimates so you can compare prices.

- Remember to get a written estimate that includes a completion date for the repairs.

- Insure your antiques with a reputable company, possibly one that specializes in antiques. When the object is out of your hands, it should be covered by either your own insurance policy or that of the restorer.

ARK RESTORATION
252 West 37th Street
New York, NY 10018
212-244-1028
Fax: 212-244-1319

CENTER ART STUDIO
307 West 38th Street
New York, NY 10018
800-242-3535
Fax: 212-586-4045
www.centerart.com

CERAMIC
RESTORATIONS
224 West 29th Street
New York, NY 10001
212-564-8669
Fax: 212-843-3742

ROSINE GREEN
ASSOCIATES
89 School Street
Brookline, MA 02446
617-277-8368
Fax: 617-731-3845
By appointment only

MATTHEW HANLON
24 West 30th Street
New York, NY 10001
212-685-4531
Fax: 212-202-3712

HESS RESTORATIONS
200 Park Avenue South
New York, NY 10003
212-260-2255
Fax: 212-979-1143

AMY KALINA OBJECT
RESTORATION
917-678-4604
By appointment only

ROGER J. KROKEY
191 Cedar Heights Road
Rhinebeck, NY 12572
845-876-3753
By appointment only

SANO STUDIO
767 Lexington Avenue
New York, NY 10021
212-759-6131

The American Institute for Conservation of Historic and Artistic Works has a helpful website that can supply you with information on caring for your objects, as well as guidelines to help you select a conservator and a list of those near you.

AMERICAN INSTITUTE
FOR CONSERVATION
OF HISTORIC AND
ARTISTIC WORKS
1717 K Street, NW
Suite 200
Washington, DC 20006
202-452-9545
Fax: 202-452-9238
www.aic.stanford.edu

China Matching and Replacement Sources

These sources will help if you need to find a suitable replacement for a broken piece of china.

CHINA REPLACEMENTS
P.O. Box 508
High Ridge, MO 63049
800-562-2655
Fax: 636-376-6319
www.chinareplacements.com

EDISH
2311 Westheimer Road
Houston, TX 77098
888-767-8282
Fax: 713-521-2546
www.edish.com

JACQUELYNN'S CHINA
MATCHING SERVICE
219 North Milwaukee
Street
Milwaukee, WI 53202
800-482-8287
Fax: 414-272-0361
www.jacquelynnschinamatch.com

REPLACEMENTS LTD.
P.O. Box 26029
Greensboro, NC 27420
800-737-5223
Fax: 336-697-3100
www.replacementsltd.com

OPPOSITE: *Whoops! If you find yourself in this situation, get a really good restorer pronto.*

SILVER

It may be just a delicate sugar spoon, an engraved snuffbox, or, if you are lucky, an ornate Victorian tea service, but it seems all of us have inherited *some* piece of silver along the way. We might not use it every day and we may polish it only twice a year, but there's a reason why we continue to treasure it, savoring its past memories along with its obvious beauty.

Since 4000 B.C., when silver was mined and traded as an early form of currency, this precious metal has been treasured. But it wasn't until the Romans came along that silver's aesthetic qualities was explored, or rather, exploited. We know that wealthy Romans sipped wine from

PREVIOUS PAGE, LEFT: *Ornamental Victorian sterling napkin rings are avidly collected, and interesting examples can be found around the world.*

PREVIOUS PAGE, RIGHT: *The fun of collecting silver is all the many shapes and sizes that it comes in, not to mention its age and pedigree. If you're in Dublin, don't miss a visit to Powerscourt Townhouse Centre, where The Silver Shop resides.*

ABOVE: *Silver surprises always turn up in outdoor antiques markets—but arrive early to find the real prizes.*

OPPOSITE: *Desk accessories are collectible as well as useful. Here an embossed, silver-topped, cut-glass Victorian inkwell on a mother-of-pearl folio.*

silver goblets and relaxed on silver-coated wooden chaises—even their servants ate off silver plates. It's no surprise, then, to learn that by the fifth century, Europe's silver supply was nearly exhausted. When fresh sources were later discovered, its use was restricted to ecclesiastical purposes until the thirteenth century, when owning silver conveyed social status.

At the center of silver making were London craftsmen. In 1238 they formed the Worshipful Company of Goldsmiths, whom we can thank today when we inspect a piece of English silver, looking for hallmarks. The guild was established by goldsmiths and silversmiths to set a standard for silver, assaying every object for its silver content before leaving a hallmark, a kind of Good Housekeeping seal of approval, on it.

Since silver is such a soft metal, it's almost always alloyed with another metal for strength and durability. Sterling silver, England's goldsmiths' hall decreed, would contain 92.5 percent silver to 7.5 percent copper or 925 of 1,000 parts pure silver, a standard to which Teddy Roosevelt gave the thumbs-up in 1907, when he said that any American piece bearing the phrase "sterling" or "sterling silver" would contain the same.

Elsewhere in the world, the proportions of silver to its alloy may be somewhat different. Very often Continental pieces will be stamped 800 or 900, meaning that there are 800 or 900 parts of pure silver in the piece. Old French silver is often as high as 950 parts pure silver. Thoroughly confused? That's why, if you collect silver, it's a good idea to consult the many excellent books available, such as *Bradbury's Book of Hallmarks* (see "Suggested Reading" on page 116).

Always inspect a piece's series of hallmarks, usually grouped together on the underside or near the edge of an object. On English silver, the *standard mark* is the symbol of the lion passant, a lion walking to the left. This guarantees sterling quality. Next, look at the *date letter* or *assay mark* that indicates when it was made. A different letter of the alphabet was used for each year, surrounded by a shield or other shape. *The mark of origin* denotes where a piece was made: a leopard's head means London; an anchor, Birmingham; a crown, Sheffield. The *maker's mark* tells who made the piece, indicated by symbols or later by initials. Finally, the *duty mark,* used from 1784 to 1890, depicts the reigning monarch's head and indicates that the duty on the piece had been paid. Also note that hallmarks are sometimes faked or even transferred from one piece to another.

Knowing the difference between silver and sterling silver is just the beginning of your silver sleuthing. Add to the list *Britannia standard* (hallmarked "Britannia"), an English silver introduced in the seventeenth century that contains 95.8 percent silver to 4.2 percent copper. The Britannia standard remained in place until 1720. Note, however, that some silversmiths still work with the higher-quality Britannia standard today.

Eighteenth-century England also gave birth to an entirely new kind of silver, *Sheffield Plate,* that fused thin silver sheets over copper, thus allowing silversmiths to use less silver and make larger domestic pieces, such as tea trays and wine coolers, more accessible. Although Sheffield Plate has a lower silver content, it was often beautifully ornamented, making it labor-intensive. Today it is highly sought after in its own right.

In the nineteenth century, *silver plate* would revolutionize the silver trade with a less expensive manufacturing process in which a white base metal was dipped into a bath of silver. It was invented in England and quickly spread to the

United States and Europe because it was so affordable. Look for a manufacturer's name and these stamps on American and English silver plate to indicate electroplate (EP), electroplated nickel silver (EPNS), and electroplated Britannia metal (EPBM).

One important thing to remember, especially when shopping in England, is not to confuse the less expensive silver plate with "plate," a general term used for silver domestic wares that comes from the Spanish word for silver, *plata.* The English frequently use the term "plate" to refer to domestic silver, a family's plate, which would be of sterling quality or higher—things like candlesticks, sauceboats, tureens, and table silver passed down from one generation to the next.

Now that you're conversant in the different kinds of silver, it's important to understand the various methods used to decorate a piece.

ABOVE: *A lyrical display of silver tableware at London's Portobello Road.*

- *Engraving* is the cutting of lines and patterns into the surface of a piece. We've all seen engraved silver baby cups and monogrammed flatware. *Bright cut* is a kind of engraving that picks out tiny bits of silver while simultaneously burnishing the surface.
- *Piercing* makes perforations in the silver.
- *Chasing* is achieved with a hammer and a punch, with the silversmith working from the front or outside, resulting in raised and depressed areas that create lovely dimensions. *Flat chasing* produces decoration in very low relief.
- *Repoussé* and *embossing* are interchangeable terms that refer to a process similar to chasing except that the work is done from the inside or back of the piece for greater depth. Goblets and tea urns adorned with flowers, scrolls, and shells might be decorated with a combination of embossing and chasing.

- *Gadrooning,* a decorative raised border around the rim of a candlestick, is a type of embossing, as is *fluting,* which grooves in the opposite direction of gadrooning—in instead of out.
- *Gilding* fuses gold onto the surface of a piece, sometimes to protect it, such as the interiors of saltcellars and egg cups.

From the highly-sought-after rococo-style silver made by the French Huguenots to rare pieces of chaste American colonial silver, to England's and Europe's (think Marie Antoinette and her mother, Empress Maria Theresa) seemingly endless aristocratic commissions of exquisite toilette sets, chocolate pots, candelabra, and epergnes, silver collecting is downright addictive.

As with any antique, master your subject before you buy: The most seasoned collectors can identify their silver even *before* they inspect the hallmarks. Look for good design, fine craftsmanship, and excellent condition. Pieces should be pristine and crisp and not look worn out or be altered in any way. Excellent silver exists in every era of the craft, so no matter what you crave—Art Deco, Art Nouveau, Georgian, or Victorian—get out your magnifying glass and dictionary of hallmarks and stock up on silver polish!

SUGGESTED READING

Bradbury, Frederick. Bradbury's Book of Hallmarks. *United Kingdom: Garnder's, 2002.*

Ensko, Stephen Guernsey. American Silversmiths and Their Marks V. *Boston: David R. Godine, 1990.*

Wyler, Seymour B. Book of Old Silver: English, American, and Foreign. *New York: Crown Publishers, 1970.*

Silver will inevitably tarnish. The trick is to keep it sparkling so that it makes you smile every time you look at it.

Cleaning

- There are specific polishes for each type of metal, so be sure you know what your object is made of before attempting to clean it. Is it sterling silver, silver plate, pewter, brass, or bronze?
- Polish only when necessary. Overpolishing can prematurely wear away the crisp details of the design and obscure monograms, maker's marks, and the engraving on a piece of silver.
- Pieces that are slightly tarnished can be gently cleaned rather than polished. First dust the object lightly with a soft dusting brush or cloth, then wash it in soapy water with a mild detergent. Dry thoroughly.
- Rinse utensils immediately after a meal. Dried food—especially foods like lemons and eggs or tomatoes—can cause pitting on your silver. Silver saltcellars should always have glass liners to avoid corrosion caused by salt.
- Use a sponge to apply a nonabrasive foaming paste cleaner (like Goddard's) that will wash off easily. Use a cotton swab, never a brush, on hard-to-reach areas. Avoid the silver dip

method as it will strip the patina off the piece.
- Rinse the piece thoroughly and use a soft cotton flannel or linen cloth to dry it quickly, bringing out its natural shine.
- Wear cotton gloves to prevent marks and tarnishing caused by the oil on our skin.
- Ivory-handled knives should be hand-washed in lukewarm water and dried immediately.
- Wax the wood on the handles of teapots and coffeepots with beeswax before you begin, and try not to immerse the wood in the water.
- Candlesticks that have green felt on their bases should be immersed headfirst so as not to wet the fabric.

BELOW, LEFT: *Quick-fix silver cleaning gloves are available at most hardware stores for last-minute polishes.*

BELOW, RIGHT: *I'll rinse this piece immediately after I polish it and go on to the next.*

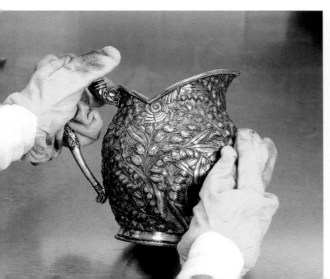

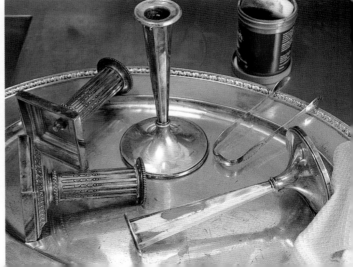

ABOVE: *Silver gems in a regal setting.*

BELOW: *A woven Victorian cutlery basket lined with baize holds a collection of serving pieces soon to be wrapped individually in brown Pacific Silvercloth before being stored.*

Storing

Before putting your silver away:

- Make sure the piece is thoroughly dry, since moisture can cause tarnishing.
- Never wrap silver in newspapers or dry-cleaning bags.
- Store your pieces in soft flannel treated with zinc, such as Pacific Silvercloth, made especially for protecting silver and slowing the rate of tarnishing. Buy the fabric by the yard and wrap each object in a cut piece, or make little bags out of it. Lined silver trays or chests are fine for storage also.

Supplies

cotton flannel "one-wipe" dust cloths, dusting brushes, Pacific Silvercloth fabric and trays

ARCHIVAL SUPPLIERS
800-628-1912
Fax: 800-532-9281
www.archivalsuppliers.com

cotton flannel or linen fabric

JO-ANN FABRICS
888-739-4120
Fax: 330-463-6670
www.joann.com

Goddard's silver polish

GODDARD'S
877-661-1853
Fax: 920-684-6573

Restorers

BRANDT & OPIS
46 West 46th Street
New York, NY 10036
212-245-9237
Fax: 212-302-0892

PAUL KARNER RESTORATION
& DESIGN STUDIO
249 East 77th Street
New York, NY 10021
Tel. and Fax: 212-517-9742

WILLIAM MANFREDI
Tel. and Fax: 212-260-5591
By appointment only

THOME SILVERSMITHS
49 West 37th Street
New York, NY 10018
212-764-5426
Fax: 570-426-7481

The American Institute for Conservation of Historic and Artistic Works has a helpful website that can supply you with information on caring for your objects, as well as guidelines to help you select a conservator and a list of those near you.

AMERICAN INSTITUTE FOR
CONSERVATION OF HISTORIC
AND ARTISTIC WORKS
1717 K Street, NW, Suite 200
Washington, DC 20006
202-452-9545
Fax: 202-452-9238
www.aic.stanford.edu

Silver Replacement Sources

Here are several sources that specialize in replacing lost or damaged silver in specific patterns.

BEVERLY BREMER SILVER SHOP
3164 Peachtree Road, NE
Atlanta, GA 30305
800-270-4009
Fax: 404-261-9709
www.beverlybremer.com

PAST PLEASURES ANTIQUES
P.O. Box 1269
Point Clear, AL 36564
Tel. and Fax: 251-928-8484
www.cyberattic.com/~/pleasures
Coin silver only

The following website lists an international directory of dealers specializing in locating hard-to-find tableware patterns.

SET YOUR TABLE
P.O. Box 22481
Lincoln, NE 68542
800-600-2127
www.setyourtable.com

GLASS

Goblets, compotes, decanters, mirrors, chandeliers, inkwells, vases, candlesticks—just think of all the glass that we live with in our homes, and when these objects are antiques, they're even more treasured, forever dazzling us with their history and their fragile beauty.

"And all around the table were the Chinese cups, the stemmed glasses for the Frontignan wine, and in the middle, the cake flavored with rum," Colette wrote contentedly in her journal. I know exactly how she felt stepping away and admiring her table. I often do the same, because I love welcoming guests with a table set with my antique china and glassware.

It was an Egyptian artisan in 2500 B.C. who first thought to fashion a molten mixture of silica (sand) and alkali into vessels to hold perfume and oil. The Romans invented the glass blowpipe, a hollow rod through which a glassmaker could blow to transform a molten ball at the other end into something exquisite. After blowing the piece, the maker would transfer it to a pontil rod for further shaping. When removed, the pontil left a mark; if we spot an old pontil mark today, it's sometimes a clue that we're looking at a piece of free-blown glass, the medium's earliest and rarest form.

Some of the world's most magnificent glass came from Murano, Venice, which ruled as the center of glassmaking as early as the thirteenth century. Venetian craftsmen were master blowers, adding metal oxides to the glass to produce brilliant enameled colors. By the fifteenth century, they had also perfected *cristallo,* clear glass (hence the name crystal), and the production of mirrors. Venetian glassblowers were so valued that they were forbidden to leave the city, although some did escape, settling in Bohemia, which would become famous for its own flashed glass. Some glassblowers made it to other parts of Europe, where the glass they produced was dubbed *façon de Venise,* or "in the Venetian style."

From the Islamic Middle East throughout Europe, artisans continued to develop different glassmaking techniques and perfect its magnificent ornamentation. Adding to free-blown glass, these makers developed the two other primary methods for producing glassware.

Blown molded glass was, as you would guess, blown into a mold, cooled, then removed with the imprint of a pattern. How can you tell if you're looking at blown molded glass? Look for seam lines that once joined to the mold.

PREVIOUS PAGE, LEFT: *Strikingly sleek glass from the 1940s works today in all types of settings.*

PREVIOUS PAGE, RIGHT: *Glass goes with everything; its transparency only flatters its companions. Here a collection of inlaid tortoiseshell tea caddies and cut-glass boxes and tumblers reside in front of pressed-glass dessert plates from the 1800s.*

ABOVE: *How many ways can they design a glass goblet? Ones like these, handblown on the Venetian island of Murano in the nineteenth century, are still being made in the same style today for lucky shoppers like us.*

Pressed glass was invented in the nineteenth century. This efficient method of pouring molten glass into an intricately carved mold, then pressing it with a weight, revolutionized glassmaking, eliminating the time-intensive handblowing process and paving the way for commercial glass production. The Boston and Sandwich Glass Works is among the best-known manufacturers of pressed glass.

Aficionados of antique glass choose an object for a variety of reasons, including age, design, shape, or function. Some are attracted to colored glass, which is made by adding various metal oxides. Post–Civil War ruby glass, the creamy opaque quality of milk glass, the silvery luster of mercury glass, and the literal yellow-greenish glow of Vaseline glass are all examples of this. Color threaded with distinctive white swirls and stripes indicates another collectible category, English Nailsea and Italian *latticino* glass. In cameo glass, dark-colored glass serves as a background, while an outer layer of a lighter color is carved away to mimic the look of a cameo.

Such was the appeal of colored glass that artists adopted it as a medium and thus was nineteenth-century art glass born. Created purely for decoration, this glass is a favorite collectible of antiques lovers. Amberina, Burmese, and Peachblow are all shaded bicolor kinds of art glass, usually noted by a white lining. Iridescent glass, marked by its rainbowlike surface, is one of the most collected forms, including the works of its best known maker, Louis Comfort Tiffany, whose Favrile "peacock" glass is truly unforgettable.

While color may have added enchantment to glass, substances like flint and lead created a different kind of beauty, a perfect transparence and weight that allow for spectacular cutting, slicing, and scalloping facets. Flint glass and lead crystal production flourished in eighteenth-century England and Ireland and was widely imitated, especially in the United States. Today this beautiful cut glass is highly valued, commanding impressive prices at auction.

Ornamentation is another area that attracts the keen attention of a collector. Since the early Egyptians, glassmakers have adorned their works with inlay and overlay techniques, filigree, gilding, and enamels. Glass can be embellished in many ways—*cutting,* when grinding the surface produces the geometric patterns we find in English and American lead crystal; *engraving,* when a diamond point or a copper wheel cuts words, names, or initials into the glass (*relief, stipple,* and *intaglio* are kinds of engraving); *frosting,* when acid or sandblasting produces a frosted-glass appearance; and *enameling,* when color is fused onto the surface to look as if it were painted on, as we might find in a church's stained-glass windows.

Indeed, glass collecting is an endlessly fascinating pursuit, and the third most popular area of collecting among Americans. My recent conversations with dealers and collectors suggest that it's not just rare early glass and old mirrors that antiques lovers are snapping up but overlooked categories like Venetian glass, 1930s and 1940s French perfume bottles, 1950s cocktailware, 1960s glassware, and American brilliant-cut glass, carnival glass (whose iridescence earned it the nickname "poor man's Tiffany"), and crackle glass. Other shoppers are devoted to a particular glassmaker, such as Tiffany or the Art Nouveau masters Eugene Rousseau and Emile Gallé.

No matter what kind of glass is your weakness, be wise when you buy. Remember that even the tiniest damage devalues a piece of glass, so inspect the piece carefully, especially at the base of a handle or stem, where pressure can be strongest. Cultivate the "feel" of old glass, a certain velvety patina. Look for mottling in old mirrors, and, as always, search for signs of wear, little random scratches underneath the base of the piece from decades of being moved about. Also inspect for a pontil mark, though this shouldn't be relied upon as an infallible test of age because some old makers ground off their pontils on pieces of fine glass such as paperweights, while some modern producers may have left them on. Remember, glass has been reproduced and old forms copied since those early Egyptians started it all, so read up on your favorite types of glass *before* you go shopping.

SUGGESTED READING

Battie, David, and Simon Cottle, eds. Sotheby's Concise Encyclopedia of Glass. *London: Conran Octopus, 1991.*

Kampfer, Fritz, and Klaus G. Beyer. Glass: A World History. *New York: New York Graphic Society, 1966.*

Moore, N. Hudson. Old Glass: European and American. *New York: Tudor, 1935.*

Spillman, Jane Shadel. Glassmaking: America's First Industry. *Corning, N.Y.: Corning Museum of Glass, 1976.*

The magical qualities of glass, its fragile delicacy and beauty, make caring for it a labor of love. The following are some tips that will make that labor a little easier.

Cleaning

- Set aside ample time for washing your glass objects.
- Always wash your antique glasses by hand, never in a dishwasher.
- To avoid chipping and breakage, use a towel to cover your work surface and line the sink in case something slips out of your hands. I like to place a separate plastic bowl in the sink for washing.
- Fill the sink with lukewarm water and a mild detergent like Ivory dishwashing liquid. If the glass is especially greasy, add a few tablespoons of vinegar to the water to cut the grease.
- Wash only one piece at a time, supporting it from the bottom with both hands. Slip it into the water sideways to prevent sudden expansion. And remember, glass is transparent and hard to see, especially when submerged in clear water.
- Rinse thoroughly to avoid leaving any soapy residue.
- Glass will become cloudy if it is not completely dried when put away. Nothing beats a traditional 100-percent-linen "glass cloth" for drying a piece thoroughly. If glass develops "bloom" or a cloudy discoloration (referred to as "sick" glass) there is nothing you can do but take it to an expert, who can sometimes reverse the problem.
- Repaired glass should never be soaked in water as it may come unglued.

- Decanters need special attention. When storing them, always remove the stoppers, never using force to free a jammed stopper. Decanters should be dried upside down to prevent watermarks on the bottom.
- Mirrors can be cleaned using a mild cleaner like Windex sprayed on a wad of cotton instead of a cloth. By using this technique, you can avoid damaging the frame.

Storing

Storing glass properly is crucial.
- Avoid accidents by putting only one piece away at a time.
- An ideal spot for storing glassware is a cabinet with a door to help keep dust at bay.
- Objects placed too close together could vibrate, hitting one another and shattering.
- Place objects well back from the edge of a shelf, with small ones in front of larger ones.
- Do not store glass in newspapers or tissue paper, which attract humidity.

BELOW: *Gently sponge one item of glass at a time so that you don't risk any accidents.*

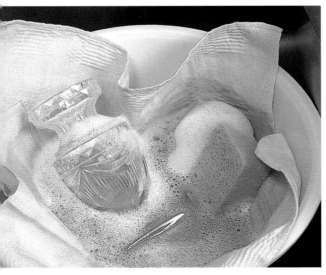

Supplies

linen glass cloths

GRACIOUS HOME
1220 Third Avenue
New York, NY 10021
212-517-6300
Fax: 212-988-8990
www.gracioushome.com

WILLIAMS-SONOMA
877-812-6235
Fax: 702-363-2541
www.williams-sonoma.com

Restorers

CENTER ART STUDIO
307 West 38th Street
New York, NY 10018
800-242-3535
Fax: 212-586-4045
www.centerart.com

GLASS RESTORATIONS
1597 York Avenue
New York, NY 10028
Tel. and Fax: 212-517-3287

ROSINE GREEN
ASSOCIATES
89 School Street
Brookline, MA 02446

617-277-8368
Fax: 617-731-3845
By appointment only

HESS RESTORATIONS
200 Park Avenue South
New York, NY 10003
212-260-2255
Fax: 212-979-1143

ANTON LAUB GLASS
35 Westervelt Place
Cresskill, NJ 07626
201-871-3663
Fax: 201-871-3692
By appointment only

The American Institute for Conservation of Historic and Artistic Works has a helpful website that can supply you with information on caring for your objects, as well as guidelines to help you select a conservator and a list of those near you.

AMERICAN INSTITUTE
FOR CONSERVATION
OF HISTORIC AND
ARTISTIC WORKS
1717 K Street, NW
Suite 200
Washington, DC 20006
202-452-9545
Fax: 202-452-9238
www.aic.stanford.edu

BELOW: *American pedestal cake plates being dried with a linen glass cloth before storage.*

TEXTILES

Of all the lovely things I've acquired over the years, antique textiles are still my first passion. Maybe it's because of the beautiful handmade clothes with which my grandmother spoiled me, or perhaps it resulted from my years in fashion, spent covering the Italian and French runways, but I can honestly say that after all this time, my love for beautiful antique fabrics—lace, quilts, needlework, early remnants of old silks, and everything in between—still rages on.

Over the past twenty-five years, the antique textile market has exploded. Auction houses now devote individual sales to costume and

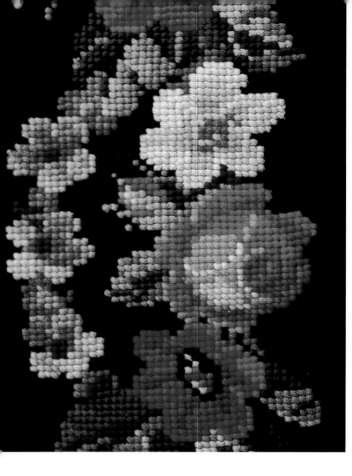

PREVIOUS PAGE, LEFT: *Collecting antique clothing and accessories can be fun because you're always coming across the unexpected. These early gold-brocaded silk slippers beckoned to me in Paris's Vanves flea market.*

PREVIOUS PAGE, RIGHT: *A sampling of the eighteenth-century toile de Jouy bed hangings that I've managed to find over the years.*

ABOVE: *A detail of a Victorian bell-pull needlepointed in wool.*

OPPOSITE: *I like to think about who may have stitched this intricately embroidered shawl. She must have been a keen gardener—just look at all the different flowers!*

textiles, interior decorators use old fabrics in their designs, and Oscar nominees regularly waltz down the red carpet in vintage couture gowns. Because the category is so broad, I can offer only an *amuse bouche* here, but I urge you to research your area of interest; start with the "Suggested Reading" list on page 130.

Though historians can't quite decide when our ancestors shed their animal pelts and began twining and weaving threads, the oldest European fragments date from about 4600 B.C. We do know that from its earliest days fabric was very precious, used and reused in every way. Even Mary Queen of Scots snapped up monks' old vestments for bed hangings in her boudoir—my kind of girl.

We also know that the eighteenth century brought the flying shuttle for weaving large pieces of cloth and the spinning jenny for spinning yarn, and, in the nineteenth century, the Jacquard loom was introduced for large-scale production. In many cases, textiles were young girls' and women's work, which, in some way, makes collecting the surviving bits all the more poignant.

Let's start with the various types of needlework that were used as decoration in the home from the seventeenth through the nineteenth centuries. *Samplers,* colored linen or silk threads embroidered on linen backgrounds, were originally records of the many stitches and techniques used in sewing. These highly prized decorative panels were frequently signed and dated by the young girls who made them to show their skill and proficiency as needlewomen. Samplers are beautiful, complex, personal pieces of history and are very valuable today, especially those made in colonial America. *Silk work,* made from silk threads embroidered on a silk background, is one of the most elegant types of needlework. The subtle, painting-like scenes often stitched on mourning pictures are one example. *Stump work,* popular in late-seventeenth-century England and also called *raised work,* has a three-dimensional quality. Design elements were stuffed and stood in relief on an embroidered scene, a technique that was used on jewel caskets and picture frames. *Crewel work* was done with richly colored twisted wool thread, usually in bold floral patterns on larger pieces such as bed hangings and curtains in the late seventeenth to early eighteenth centuries. *Beadwork* incorporates tiny colored glass beads in the decoration of small objects, such as reticules and sewing accessories, popular in the seventeenth century and again in the nineteenth century. *White work* is white embroidery on delicate white fabric—think of fine nineteenth-century batiste christening gowns and handkerchiefs. Finally, *needlepoint,* a series of wool or silk stitches worked on a canvas backing, was done extensively in the Victorian era to cover pillows, footstools, bellpulls, slippers, cigar cases, and anything else you could imagine. *Berlin wool work* is a type of needlepoint that any unsophisticated needlewoman could do and came at the end of the needlepoint craze.

While we are discussing needlepoint we shouldn't overlook *passementerie,* ornate trimmings, including tassels, fringes, braids, beads, and gimps first used in the seventeenth century. We think of them ornamenting the richly upholstered furniture, bed hangings, and cushions in the courts of the French kings and stately homes such as Knole or Osterley Park in England. There is no English word for *passementerie* because these beautiful bits of froufrou were originally created in France and are very much in fashion now if you are lucky enough to find them.

Another notable antique textile is *lace,* which is

basically a type of embroidery. First made in Italy and Flanders in the fifteenth century, it has been highly valued throughout the ages. There are two types: *needle lace,* which is made with a single needle and thread, and *bobbin lace,* which is sometimes called *pillow lace,* because it's created using a pillow in which pins passed through a paper pattern are weighted with numerous wood, ivory, or metal bobbins wound with thread. There are hundreds of lace designs, which makes the subject a rich and sometimes confusing one. Stunning lace pieces that survive from before the nineteenth century, such as liturgical garments, collars, cuffs, handkerchiefs, and veils, are rare and highly sought after.

Quilts are an enduring American tradition. Created by stitching together three separate layers of fabric in a variety of styles, they were made in

Europe from the seventeenth century. Breathtakingly intricate, they became popular in eighteenth-century America and often reflected the lives of the women who made them. Their decorative and historical importance makes them prized by collectors and museums.

Not all antique textiles were made with the needle; many came off the loom. Among them are works literally worthy of royals—tapestries. In the Middle Ages they were used to warm up and cover the usually dirty walls of damp castles and manor houses. Tapestries are intricate, painstaking works of art, typically produced in northern France and Belgium in the sixteenth and seventeenth centuries. Gobelin, Beauvais, and Aubusson are names we associate with them.

Also off the loom are printed fabrics, which are becoming ever more collectible—it's not unusual for avid collectors to buy mere swatches of a rare piece. Some of the earliest of these are woodblock-printed cottons such as toiles de Jouy produced around 1760 by Christoph-Philippe Oberkampf in France. Calicoes and the repeat patterns of antique chintzes are also prized, along with pre-nineteenth-century printed fabrics created with rollers or copper plates and twentieth-century Art Deco patterns.

Upon inheriting her family home, Mirador, interior designer Nancy Lancaster wrote that she ordered "new upholstery and curtains to be made of different patterns and colors of chintz, which was quite a step in the twenties. But only *old* chintz. Old chintz fit the mood of the house; I wanted the feeling that it hadn't been decorated at all, just lived in." One can just imagine how beautiful it must have looked with all that lovely old fabric.

True aficionados do not limit their collections to their homes. They also snap up antique garments, not always for their wearability but for their sheer beauty and workmanship. From the simple cloaks of the nineteenth-century Shakers, to the magnificent embroidered shawls of Kashmir, to opulent silk Chinese robes, to the delicate folds of a fin de siècle Fortuny dress, antique clothing is one of the fastest-growing areas of textile collecting. Indeed, as time marches on, the vintage clothing market is always growing, so dig out those old Puccis, Ossie Clarks, Chanels, and Saint Laurents and make sure you have them properly stored—they're getting more valuable every day!

SUGGESTED READING

Ames, Frank. Kashmir Shawl. *Woodbridge, England: Antique Collectors Club, 1986.*

Bonneville, Françoise de. The Book of Fine Linen. *Paris: Flammarion, 1994.*

Montgomery, Florence. Printed Textiles. *New York: Viking, 1970.*

Priest, Alan. Costumes from the Forbidden City. *New York: Arno Press, 1974.*

Reighe, Emily. An Illustrated Guide to Lace. *Woodbridge, England: Antique Collectors Club, 1986.*

Ring, Betty. American Needlework Treasures. *New York: E. P. Dutton, 1987.*

Swan, Susan Burrows. Plain and Fancy. *New York: Holt, Rinehart and Winston, 1977.*

Christening gowns, quilts, embroidered cloths, delicate handkerchiefs, and samplers are just some of the most cherished possessions passed down in a family from one generation to the next—also the most vulnerable. With a little extra care, these items will survive for generations to come.

Cleaning

- Old fabrics and lace are extremely fragile. You can irreparably damage a piece by cleaning it improperly. Consult a textile expert if you have any questions.
- Do not use a washing machine. Wash old bed and table linens by hand in lukewarm water with a mild detergent like Orvus WA Paste or Ivory Flakes. If the item is too large to wash by hand, send it to a fine hand laundry that specializes in old linens.
- Always be sure to rinse items thoroughly in clear water. Do not wring or twist them because they can tear easily when wet.
- If your antique linens acquire new stains like red wine, tea, or coffee, the stain should be blotted, not rubbed. Immediately hold the stain under cold running water until it fades slightly, then bring the item to a fine hand laundry.
- Chlorine bleach is destructive to all old fabrics and should never be used.
- Do not hang wet pieces on a line to dry, as the weight of the water and gravity could cause the fabric to tear. Dry wet items flat on a clean white cotton towel, out of direct sunlight.
- Place delicate lace pieces in a net bag before washing very carefully by hand.
- Old lace can be extremely valuable, so if you have any questions about cleaning it, consult an expert first.

- Colored textiles such as quilts should be handled carefully. Colors may not be permanent and could bleed. Always talk to a textile conservator before washing or cleaning any colored textile of value.
- Handle vintage clothing with tender loving care. Use the services of a fine cleaner.
- A small, handheld, low-power vacuum usually works well for removing surface dust from needlework pillows and upholstered pieces.
- Antique carpets should be professionally cleaned by a reputable company.

Storing

To protect your fragile textiles:
- Keep them out of direct sunlight and fluorescent light, which can fade colors and accelerate deterioration.
- Use ultraviolet-proof Plexiglas and acid-free mats when having old textiles framed.
- All textiles should be as clean as possible when stored away. Old starch and dirt will make a piece even more fragile and damage it.
- Wrap folded textiles in unbuffered acid-free tissue. Always stuff a piece of tissue inside the folds to prevent deep, permanent creasing. Refold the item periodically.
- Always store antique textiles flat, never on hangers. Fold or roll your wrapped pieces in acid-free boxes. Try not to overcrowd them.

- Roll large pieces like quilts on acid-free tubes and wrap them in a clean white cotton sheet.
- Keep your boxes in a well-ventilated place where the temperature and relative humidity are moderate. Rapid changes in humidity, either up or down, can cause fibers to break down.
- Pesticides and mothballs damage old textiles.

Supplies

Orvus WA paste, textile storage boxes, unbleached cotton cloth, unbuffered acid-free tissue

ARCHIVAL SUPPLIERS
800-628-1912
Fax: 800-532-9281
www.archivalsuppliers.com

Restorers

antique textiles

GINA BIANCO TEXTILE &
COSTUME CONSERVATION
212-924-1685
By appointment only

LINENS LIMITED
240 North Milwaukee Street
Milwaukee, WI 53202
800-637-6334
Fax: 414-223-1126
thelaundryat.com

ABOVE: *Nothing looks as beautiful as a stack of crisp, freshly ironed antique linens.*

BELOW: *I roll my antique cloths in acid-free tissue before tucking them away into acid-free boxes.*

OPPOSITE: *Keep an eye out for fragments of eighteenth- and nineteenth-century printed chintz textiles. They've become very sought after.*

TEXTILE CONSERVATION WORKSHOP
3 Main Street
South Salem, NY 10590
914-763-5805
Fax: 914-763-5549
www.rap-arcc.org/tcwsite

antique carpets

HARRY EKIZIAN
34 East 29th Street
New York, NY 10016
212-683-1055

F. J. HAKIMIAN
136 East 57th Street
New York, NY 10022
212-371-6900
Fax: 212-753-0277
www.fjhakimian.com

LONG ISLAND CARPET CLEANERS
301 Norman Avenue
Brooklyn, NY 11222
800-635-0058
Fax: 718-389-9152
www.liccarpetcleaners.com

*hand-laundering and dry-cleaning for
fine linens and vintage clothing*

FASHION AWARD CLEANERS
1462 Lexington Avenue
New York, NY 10128
212-289-5623

HALLAK CLEANERS
1232 Second Avenue
New York, NY 10021
212-879-4694

MEURICE GARMENT CARE
245 East 57th Street
New York, NY 10022
800-240-3377
www.garmentcare.com

The American Institute for Conservation of Historic
and Artistic Works has a helpful website that can supply
you with information on caring for your objects, as well
as guidelines to help you select a conservator and a list
of those near you.

AMERICAN INSTITUTE FOR CONSERVATION OF
HISTORIC AND ARTISTIC WORKS
1717 K Street, NW, Suite 200
Washington, DC 20006
202-452-9545
Fax: 202-452-9238
www.aic.stanford.edu

ANTIQUING

AROUND THE WORLD

When I was in the fashion business, I went to the couture and ready-to-wear collections in Europe each season. It sounds glamorous, but it was hectic, hard work—racing from one end of the city to the other covering the shows and doing paperwork until the wee hours. My indulgence was going to the flea markets on the weekends. Foraging in the Marché aux Puces in Paris and London's Camden Passage started me on a collecting binge that transformed my life. In fact, I started my New York City shop, Cherchez, with all the antiques I found—from porcelain plates and silver tableware to pristine Victorian bed linens and Fortuny dresses. Even though I no longer have the shop, I can't break the habit!

This section contains all you need to get started (or continue) your collecting in some of the most exciting cities in the world. All of my insider sources are here, from antiques shops and auctions to antiques shows and flea markets—with the critical details, like the times to go for the best pickings. In addition, I've included lists of favorite unique museums and historic homes. I'm always inspired when I visit these places—and I come home with some terrific ideas, too.

My husband and I have been traveling for many years and not everywhere we've stayed or dined has been perfect. So the places I'm sharing with you here are tried-and-true and I've enjoyed going to them again and again. This doesn't mean you shouldn't go exploring on your own. I hope you will, and that you'll let me know if you find some other wonderful places that can be added to my lists.

Bon voyage!

PREVIOUS PAGE: *"Game of Round the World With Nellie Bly" (McLoughlin Brothers, 1890).*

OPPOSITE: *Glamorous 1920s luggage labels.*

NEW YORK CITY & U.S. COUNTRY MARKETS

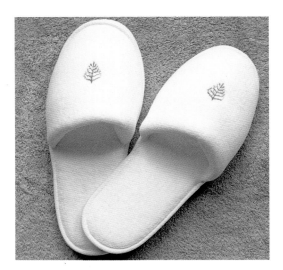

My hometown is a constantly changing work in progress that has always been an antiques collector's paradise—a center of the art and antiques world. There is more of everything here—a constantly changing landscape of new and old places, on and off the beaten path. When you are planning an antiques-shopping spree to New York City, remember the following: Take your vitamins, wear comfortable shoes, and pack your credit cards before you come to visit the most exciting city in the world.

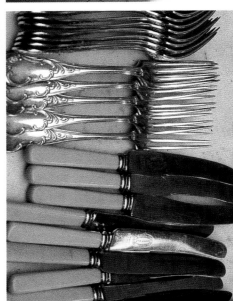

Antiques Shops

New York City has hundreds of wonderful antiques shops. There are so many good ones that you'll want to visit as many as possible. You'll find everything from charming antique buttons to dramatic pieces of elegant furniture and an astonishing array of decorative accessories. New York is such a big city that it makes sense to organize your visits by geographical location. So you can do this sensibly, I have divided the following list into shops that are uptown or downtown.

Most of the uptown shops are situated on the Upper East Side, off Madison Avenue starting at 57th Street. Those downtown are grouped in areas like Greenwich Village (on 10th and 12th Streets off University Place), Tribeca (on Duane Street), and SoHo (below Houston on the side streets between West Broadway and Lafayette Street). The shops downtown open and close later than the ones uptown, so try to call ahead.

uptown

DIDIER AARON
32 East 67th Street
212-988-5248

À LA VIEILLE RUSSIE
781 Fifth Avenue
212-752-1727

MARVIN ALEXANDER
315 East 62nd Street
212-838-2320

ALEXANDER GALLERY
942 Madison Avenue
212-472-1636

W. GRAHAM ARADER III
29 East 72nd Street
212-628-3668

ARGOSY BOOK STORE
116 East 59th Street
212-753-4455

ASPREY & GARRARD
725 Fifth Avenue
212-688-1811

BARDITH
901 Madison Avenue
212-737-3775

BETTY JANE BART
ANTIQUES
1225 Madison Avenue
212-410-2702

BAUMAN RARE BOOKS
Waldorf-Astoria
301 Park Avenue
212-759-8300

BERRY-HILL GALLERIES
11 East 70th Street
212-744-2300

GERALD BLAND
1262 Madison Avenue
212-987-8505

VOJTECH BLAU
41 East 57th Street
212-249-4525

BLUMKA GALLERIES
209 East 72nd Street
212-734-3222

YALE R. BURGE
ANTIQUES
315 East 62nd Street
212-838-4005

G. K. S. BUSH
16 East 80th Street
212-432-5289

LEE CALICCHIO
134 East 70th Street
212-717-4417

RALPH M. CHAIT
12 East 56th Street
212-758-0937

CHINESE PORCELAIN
COMPANY
475 Park Avenue
212-838-7744

DALVA BROTHERS
44 East 57th Street
212-758-2297

CAROLE DAVENPORT
131 East 83rd Street
212-734-4859

DEVENISH & COMPANY
929 Madison Avenue
212-535-2888

DK ANTIQUES
1300 Madison Avenue
212-534-8532

DAVID DUNCAN
ANTIQUES
227 East 60th Street
212-688-0666

ANDRE EMMERICH
GALLERIES
41 East 57th Street
212-752-0124

WALLY FINDLAY
GALLERIES
14 East 60th Street
212-421-5390

LAURA FISHER
ANTIQUES & QUILTS
1050 Second Avenue
212-838-2596

FLYING CRANES
ANTIQUES
1050 Second Avenue
212-223-4600

E & J FRANKEL
1040 Madison Avenue
212-879-5733

MALCOLM FRANKLIN
12 East 97th Street
212-369-0790

BARRY FRIEDMAN
32 East 67th Street
212-794-8950

GARDEN ROOM
1179 Lexington Avenue
212-879-1179

GEORGE D. GLAZER
28 East 72nd Street
212-535-5706

GODEL & COMPANY
FINE ART
39 East 72nd Street
212-288-7272

PREVIOUS PAGE, TOP ROW, LEFT TO RIGHT: *Uptown landmarks: Central Park, Rockefeller Center, Fifth Avenue.*

MIDDLE ROW, LEFT TO RIGHT: *Snapshots of the West 26th Street Flea Market, inside and out.*

BOTTOM ROW, LEFT TO RIGHT: *What treasures will we find today?*

F. GOREVIC & SON
118 East 57th Street
212-753-9319

HAMMER GALLERIES
33 West 57th Street
212-644-4400

HIRSCHL & ADLER
21 East 70th Street
212-535-8810

LIZA HYDE ANTIQUES
565 Park Avenue
212-752-3581

JAMES II GALLERIES
11 East 57th Street
212-355-7040

R. KALLER-KIMCHE
23 East 74th Street
212-288-5698

LEO KAPLAN
114 East 57th Street
212-355-7212

KENNEDY GALLERIES
730 Fifth Avenue
212-541-9600

LEIGH KENO AMERICAN
ANTIQUES
980 Madison Avenue
212-734-2381

ALICE KWARTLER
ANTIQUES
123 East 57th Street
212-752-3590

L'ANTIQUAIRE & THE
CONNOISSEUR
36 East 73rd Street
212-517-9176

L'ART DE VIVRE
978 Lexington Avenue
212-734-3510

FRED LEIGHTON
773 Madison Avenue
212-288-1872

BERNARD & S. DEAN
LEVY
24 East 84th Street
212-628-7088

MACKLOWE GALLERY
667 Madison Avenue
212-644-6400

MALMAISON ANTIQUES
253 East 74th Street
212-288-7569

MANHATTAN ART &
ANTIQUE CENTER
1050 Second Avenue
212-355-4400

J. MAVEC & COMPANY
946 Madison Avenue
212-517-7665

JUDITH AND JAMES
MILNE
506 East 74th Street
212-472-0107

ANN MORRIS ANTIQUES
239 East 60th Street
212-755-3308

NAGA ANTIQUES
145 East 61st Street
212-593-2788

NESLE
151 East 57th Street
212-755-0515

NEWEL ART GALLERIES
425 East 53rd Street
212-758-1970

OLD VERSAILLES
315 East 62nd Street
212-421-3663

FLORIAN PAPP
962 Madison Avenue
212-288-6770

AMY PERLIN ANTIQUES
306 East 61st Street
212-593-5756

KENNETH W. RENDELL
ANTIQUES
989 Madison Avenue
212-717-1776

JAMES ROBINSON
480 Park Avenue
212-752-6166

JOHN ROSSELLI
INTERNATIONAL
225 East 72nd Street
212-772-2137

ROYAL ATHENA
GALLERIES
153 East 57th Street
212-355-2034

SALANDER-O'REILLY
GALLERIES
20 East 79th Street
212-879-6606

FREDERICK SCHULTZ
41 East 57th Street
212-758-6007

SENTIMENTO
306 East 61st Street
212-750-3111

S. J. SHRUBSOLE
104 East 57th Street
212-753-8920

SPANIERMAN GALLERY
45 East 58th Street
212-832-0208

SUCHOW & SEIGEL
ANTIQUES
1050 Second Avenue
212-888-3489

URSUS BOOKS & PRINTS
Carlyle Hotel
981 Madison Avenue
212-772-8787

EARLE D. VANDEKAR
305 East 61st Street
212-308-2022

WARD & COMPANY
962 Park Avenue
212-327-4400

EDITH WEBER &
ASSOCIATES
994 Madison Avenue
212-570-9668

DORIS WEINER
1001 Fifth Avenue
212-772-8631

S. WYLER
INCORPORATED
941 Lexington Avenue
212-879-9848

RICHARD YORK
GALLERY
21 East 65th Street
212-772-9155

downtown

ANTIQUARIUS
474 Broome Street
212-343-0311

BURDEN & IZETT
180 Duane Street
212-941-8257

CAP-SUD
50 Bond Street
212-260-9114

JACQUES CARCANAGUES
106 Spring Street
212-925-8110

VICTOR CARL
ANTIQUES
55 East 13th Street
212-673-8740

CHAMELEON
231 Lafayette Street
212-343-9197

PHILIP COLLECK LTD.
830 Broadway
212-505-2500

COMING TO AMERICA
276 Lafayette Street
212-343-2968

CRANBERRY HOLE
ROAD
252 Lafayette Street
212-334-0034

DUANE
176 Duane Street
212-625-8066

GALERIE DE BEYRIE
393 West Broadway
212-219-9565

GALERIE DE FRANCE
184 Duane Street
212-965-0969

GARY'S ON 4TH
124 East 4th Street
212-473-3558

BERND GOECKLER
ANTIQUES
30 East 10th Street
212-777-8209

GRAY GARDENS
461 Broome Street
212-966-7116

JOHN J. GREDLER
ANTIQUES
110 West 25th Street
212-337-3667

HISTORICAL
MATERIALISM
125 Crosby Street
212-431-3424

HYDE PARK ANTIQUES
836 Broadway
212-477-0033

HOWARD KAPLAN
ANTIQUES
827 Broadway
212-674-1000

KARL KEMP &
ASSOCIATES
36 East 10th Street
212-254-1877

KENSINGTON PLACE
ANTIQUES
80 East 11th Street
212-533-7652

KENTSHIRE GALLERIES
37 East 12th Street
212-673-6644

JOHN KOCH ANTIQUES
514 West 24th Street
212-243-8625

EILEEN LANE ANTIQUES
150 Thompson Street
212-475-2988

LITTLE ANTIQUE SHOP
44 East 11th Street
212-673-5173

H. M. LUTHER ANTIQUES
61 East 11th Street
212-505-1485

MAISON GERARD
53 East 10th Street
212-674-7611

SUSAN MEISEL
133 Prince Street
212-254-0137

MOOD INDIGO
181 Prince Street
212-254-1176

OLD PRINT SHOP
150 Lexington Avenue
212-683-3950

O'SULLIVAN ANTIQUES
51 East 10th Street
212-260-8985

SUSAN PARRISH
ANTIQUES
390 Bleecker Street
212-645-5020

RETRO-MODERN
58 East 11th Street
212-674-0530

REYMER-JOURDAN
ANTIQUES
43 East 10th Street
212-674-4470

RITTER ANTIK
35 East 10th Street
212-673-2213

SECOND CHILDHOOD
283 Bleecker Street
212-989-6140

SECOND HAND ROSE
270 Lafayette Street
212-393-9002

SEIDENBERG
36 East 12th Street
212-260-2810

NIALL SMITH
344 Bleecker Street
212-255-0660

DAVID STYPMANN
192 Sixth Avenue
212-226-5717

T & K FRENCH
ANTIQUES
200 Lexington Avenue
212-213-2470

TUDOR ROSE
28 East 10th Street
212-677-5239

BRIAN WINDSOR
272 Lafayette Street
212-274-0411

WYETH
151 Franklin Street
212-925-5278

Antiques Shows

All year long there are wonderful antiques shows in New York. As I write this there are five outstanding shows going on from one end of the city to the other. Sometimes it's hard to get to them
all. Here are some that I think shouldn't be missed.

THE ART SHOW

Art Dealers Association of America
575 Madison Avenue
212-940-8925
The Art Show includes engravings, paintings, and
sculpture by artists from Rembrandt to Andy Warhol.

INTERNATIONAL FINE ART AND
ANTIQUES DEALERS SHOW

Haughton Fairs
220 West 93rd Street
212-877-0202
The International Fine Art and Antiques Dealers
Show is organized by Brian and Anna Haughton, who

are known for their upscale shows in London. The
merchandise is top-drawer and the international dealers exhibit a particularly fine selection of antique
furniture from here and abroad. The Haughtons also
organize the Asian Art Fair and Fine Art Fair in New
York City.

NEW YORK CERAMICS FAIR

Caskey-Lees/Sha-Dor
301-933-6994
www.caskeylees.com
The New York Ceramics Fair focuses on ceramics and
glass for the antiques connoisseur, with some fine contemporary works thrown in for good measure.

TRIPLE PIER ANTIQUES SHOW

Stella Show Management
147 West 24th Street
212-255-0020
www.stellashows.com

The Triple Pier Antiques Show is an extravaganza that takes place twice a year at the Passenger Ship Terminal Piers on the West Side of Manhattan in 200,000 square feet of space. Though heavy on collectibles and vintage, there are more than six hundred exhibitors with something for everyone. Stella Shows also presents, in conjunction with the Horticultural Society of New York, the Gramercy Garden Antiques Show, featuring approximately a hundred exhibitors of fine antique garden furniture, charming planters, accessories, and architectural ornaments.

WINTER ANTIQUES SHOW

718-292-7392
www.winterantiquesshow.com

January is the time for sophisticated collectors to attend the prestigious Winter Antiques Show at the Armory. Originally focusing on Americana, this important fifty-year-old show launches the winter social season in New York City. It now has an international flavor with some of the world's top antiques dealers creating an incredible spectacle of rare objects and furniture including jewelry, paintings, rare books, antiquities, and other unique antiques. It has been held for years in the revered Armory on 67th Street and Park Avenue, which also contains the famous Tiffany Room.

Antiques Markets

Unlike many European cities, New York has never had many outdoor markets. It's a city where vacant lots are instantly turned into skyscrapers or apartment buildings, making it difficult for these small markets to survive. However, several happy hunting grounds still exist for visitors and those savvy New Yorkers who always like a bargain.

ANNEX ANTIQUES FAIR AND MARKET

Sixth Avenue and 26th Street
212-243-5343
Saturday and Sunday, 9 A.M. to 6 P.M.

This market, sometimes called the 26th Street Flea Market, is a New York institution. Its size has been recently reduced; however, serious collectors and dealers still arrive in the early-morning hours with flashlights. *You* can get there at 9 A.M. and still find treasures—from fine to funky.

GARAGE ANTIQUES SHOW

112 West 25th Street
212-647-0707
Saturday and Sunday, 9 A.M. to 5 P.M.

Approximately 120 dealers exhibit in the Garage. Everything from old engravings to movie memorabilia is on display in a large indoor garage.

GREENFLEA MARKET

Columbus Avenue between 76th and 77th Streets
212-721-0900
Sunday, 10 A.M. to 5:30 P.M.

This indoor-outdoor market takes place in a school on the West Side of Manhattan. More than three hundred dealers sell a wide range of antiques and collectibles in addition to handmade crafts, old books, and even country-fresh produce. Vintage furniture is a specialty.

THE SHOWPLACE

40 West 25th Street
212-633-6063
Monday through Friday, 10 A.M. to 6 P.M., Saturday and Sunday, 8:30 A.M. to 5:30 P.M.

The Showplace is a group of 132 vendors displaying vintage postcards and every kind of bric-a-brac.

Auction Houses

Listed here are the top four New York City auction venues. Each has been established in the city for years and offers helpful programs for collectors, including seminars and lectures.

CHRISTIE'S
30 Rockefeller Plaza
212-636-2000
www.christies.com

DOYLE NEW YORK
175 East 87th Street
212-427-2730
www.doylenewyork.com

SOTHEBY'S
1334 York Avenue
212-606-7000
www.sothebys.com

SWANN GALLERIES
104 East 25th Street
212-254-4710
www.swanngalleries.com

Shippers

There is a great temptation to accumulate more than you should in a city that has so much to offer. The following companies will ship your antiques almost anywhere.

AIR-SEA HOUSE
40-35 22nd Street
Long Island City
718-937-6800

JAMES BOURLET/ART
LOGISTICS
38-20 Review Avenue
Long Island City
718-392-9770

FENTON/MSAS
248-06 Rockaway
  Boulevard
Jamaica
718-917-6396

FORTRESS-FAE
WORLDWIDE
49-20 5th Street
Long Island City
800-583-7661

GANDER & WHITE
21-44 44th Road
Long Island City
718-729-8877

HEDLEY'S HUMPERS
21-41 45th Road
Long Island City
718-433-4005

LOCKSON
601 Penhorn Avenue
Secaucus, NJ
201-392-9800

MARSH & MCLENNAN
1166 Avenue of the Americas
212-345-6000

Museums

I've been enjoying the city's museums since I visited them as a child with my parents, and I still haven't seen everything in them! It's hard to decide where to begin, but I would start by visiting the glorious Metropolitan Museum and then go on to some of the more intimate ones like the Forbes Galleries and the Frick Collection.

AMERICAN FOLK ART
MUSEUM
45 West 53rd Street
212-265-1040
www.folkartmuseum.org

ASIA SOCIETY
502 Park Avenue
212-517-ASIA
www.asiasociety.org

BROOKLYN MUSEUM
OF ART
200 Eastern Parkway
Brooklyn
718-638-5931
www.brooklynart.org

CHINA INSTITUTE
125 East 65th Street
212-628-4159
www.chinainstitute.org

THE CLOISTERS
Fort Tryon Park
212-923-3700
www.ny.com/museums/
  cloisters

COOPER-HEWITT
NATIONAL DESIGN
MUSEUM
2 East 91st Street
212-849-8400
www.si.edu/ndm

FORBES GALLERIES
62 Fifth Avenue
212-206-5548
www.forbes.com/
  forbescollection

FRICK COLLECTION
1 East 70th Street
212-288-0700
www.frick.org

GALLERY AT THE BARD
CENTER
18 West 86th Street
212-501-3000
www.bgc/bard.edu

INTERNATIONAL
CENTER FOR
PHOTOGRAPHY
1133 Sixth Avenue
212-860-1777
www.icp.org

JAPAN SOCIETY
333 East 47th Street
212-832-1155
www.japansociety.org

METROPOLITAN
MUSEUM
Fifth Avenue and
  82nd Street
212-535-7710
www.metmuseum.org

MORGAN LIBRARY
29 East 36th Street
212-685-0610
www.morganlibrary.org

MUSEUM OF CHINESE IN
THE AMERICAS
70 Mulberry Street
212-619-4785
www.moca-ny.org

MUSEUM OF THE CITY
OF NEW YORK
Fifth Avenue and 103rd
    Street
212-534-1672
www.mcny.org

MUSEUM AT THE
FASHION INSTITUTE OF
TECHNOLOGY
Seventh Avenue and
    27th Street
212-217-5800
www.fitnyc.suny.edu/museum

MUSEUM OF MODERN
ART
11 West 53rd Street
212-708-9400
www.moma.org

NATIONAL ACADEMY OF
DESIGN MUSEUM
1083 Fifth Avenue
212-369-4880
www.nationalacademy.org

NEUE GALERIE
1048 Fifth Avenue
212-628-6200
www.neuegalerie.org

NEW-YORK HISTORICAL
SOCIETY
2 West 77th Street
212-873-3400
www.nyhistory.org

WHITNEY MUSEUM OF
AMERICAN ART
945 Madison Avenue
212-570-3600
www.whitney.org

Organizations

Americans support a number of societies that help preserve architecture, antiques, and art in many countries of the world. Become part of the bigger picture and join some of those listed below.

AMERICAN ACADEMY
IN ROME
7 East 60th Street
New York, NY 10022
212-751-7200
Fax: 212-751-7220
www.aarome.org

AMERICAN FRIENDS OF
THE BRITISH MUSEUM
1 East 53rd Street
New York, NY 10022
212-644-0522

HISTORIC HOUSE TRUST
The Arsenal, Room 203
Central Park
New York, NY 10021
212-360-8282
www.nyc.gov/parks

IRISH GEORGIAN
SOCIETY
7 Washington Square North
New York, NY 10003
212-759-7155
www.archeire.com/igs

ROYAL OAK FOUNDATION
26 Broadway
New York, NY 10004
800-913-6565
www.royal-oak.org

SAVE VENICE
15 East 74th Street
New York, NY 10021
212-737-3141
www.savevenice.org

VERSAILLES
FOUNDATION
420 Lexington Avenue
New York, NY 10170
212-983-3436

VICTORIAN SOCIETY
205 South Camac Street
Philadelphia, PA 19107
215-545-8340

WORLD MONUMENTS
FUND
95 Madison Avenue
New York, NY 10016
646-424-9594
www.wmf.org

Hotels

New York City has so many wonderful hotels. Here's a list of some of my favorites, from the small and intimate Lowell and Mark to the Four Seasons, designed by I. M. Pei, with a sleek grandeur all its own.

THE CARLYLE
35 East 76th Street
212-744-1600
www.lhw.com/carlyle

FOUR SEASONS
57 East 57th Street
212-758-5700
www.fourseasons.com/
    newyorkfs

LOWELL
28 East 63rd Street
212-838-1400
www.lhw.com/lowellnyc

THE MARK
25 East 77th Street
212-744-4300
www.lhw.com/marknyc

THE PIERRE
Fifth Avenue and
    61st Street
212-838-8000
www.fourseasons.com/pierre

Restaurants

New Yorkers must eat out more than anyone. As a result, the city has more restaurants than any other in the world. My husband and I prefer restaurants that have a track record, friendly service, and delicious food.

BALTHAZAR
805 Spring Street
212-965-1414

BAR PITTI
268 Sixth Avenue
212-982-3300

CRAFT
43 East 19th Street
212-780-0880

DANIEL
60 East 65th Street
212-288-0033

ELEVEN MADISON PARK
11 Madison Avenue
212-889-0905

GIGINO TRATTORIA
323 Greenwich Street
212-431-1112

GOTHAM BAR & GRILL
12 East 12th Street
212-620-4020

GRAMERCY TAVERN
42 East 20th Street
212-477-0777

LA GRENOUILLE
3 East 52nd Street
212-752-1495

LE BERNARDIN
155 West 51st Street
212-489-1515

LE ZINC
139 Duane Street
212-513-0001

NOVGATINE
1 Central Park West
212-299-3900

OUEST
2315 Broadway
212-580-8700

OSTERIA DEL CIRCO
120 West 55th Street
212-265-3636

PICHOLINE
35 West 64th Street
212-724-8585

TRIBECA GRILL
375 Greenwich Street
212-941-3900

U.S. COUNTRY MARKETS

From Massachusetts to California, interior designers and antiques collectors are flocking to country markets in untold numbers. These outdoor events take place in fair grounds, fields, and parking lots throughout the year and cause many of us to behave in a most eccentric manner—arriving at the crack of dawn with cups of steaming coffee, clutching empty tote bags, flashlights at the ready. All this for the thrill of uncovering an unexpected find. At these events, the past is affordable and the fun of a day spent foraging in an open field is always worth it.

Shopping in markets as large as these can be exhausting, so plan ahead. Here are some basic tips:

- Arrive early and bring a flashlight. Get there before the crowd arrives, when the dealers are unpacking. You'll miss something if you don't.

- Find out if there is an early admission fee that will enable you to enter the show several hours before the general public.

- Go up and down each row in regular order so you don't miss any booths.

- Two pairs of eyes are better than one, so bring a friend who loves antiques as much as you do. (A friend who doesn't can be a distraction and may want to go home early, God forbid.) Cell phones help to keep in touch with each other.

- Don't forget your creature comforts—bring comfortable shoes, a jacket with lots of pockets instead of a handbag, a bottle of water, moist towelettes, sunscreen, and some fruit or cookies to keep you going (some aspirin wouldn't hurt, either).

JOE LOEHNDORF
Painting
and
Decorating

J.E. SHEEHAN
HORSE
SHOEING

P.H.
NORDLAND
JEWELER

11 12 1
10 2
9 3
8 4
7 6 5

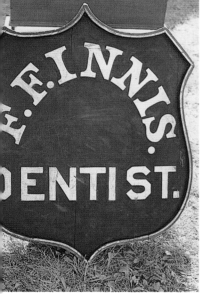

F.F. INNIS.
DENTIST.

HOTEL
GARAGE
STA
ACCOMMODA

ALL
HAIR
CUTS
25¢

UNCTURES
EPAIRED
25

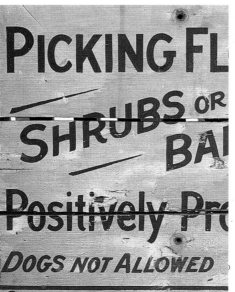

PICKING FL
SHRUBS OR
BA
Positively Pro
DOGS NOT ALLOWED

NECTAR
TEA

- Take a measuring tape and a magnifying glass for looking at hallmarks and possible repairs.

- Bring your own strong tote bags and tissue paper for wrapping breakable items.

- Bring a cart with wheels, or rent a U-Haul truck if you intend to buy, buy, buy.

- Bring cash, as most dealers will not accept credit cards and only some accept checks.

- Remember to get receipts.

- Don't be afraid to bargain. You can always ask a dealer "Can you do better?" or "Will you take less for this item?" Remember, the larger the purchase the larger the discount you're likely to get.

- Ask questions. Most dealers love to share their knowledge with collectors who care.

- Be prepared to dig—don't overlook those cartons piled up in a corner. You never know what's in the bottom of them.

- Don't be indecisive. You will forever regret not buying that one-of-a-kind object when you go back and it has already been sold.

PREVIOUS PAGE: *You can find some wonderful nostalgic handpainted signs at the country markets listed here.*

BELOW: *American Ironstone in the field on an apple-pie kinda day.*

OPPOSITE, LEFT: *Brake when you see a country scene like this.*

OPPOSITE, RIGHT: *Americana at Antiques in the Cow Pasture in Salisbury, Connecticut.*

Country Markets

arizona

PHOENIX ANTIQUE MARKET
Arizona State Fairgrounds
Phoenix
623-587-7488
www.azantiqueshow.com
Six months a year, third weekend of each month

california

LONG BEACH OUTDOOR ANTIQUE AND COLLECTIBLE MARKET
Long Beach Veteran's Stadium
Long Beach
323-655-5703
www.longbeachantique market.com
Third Sunday of each month

ROSE BOWL FLEA MARKET
Rose Bowl Parking Lot
Pasadena
323-560-7469
www.rgcshows.com
Second Sunday of each month

SANTA MONICA AIRPORT ANTIQUE AND COLLECTIBLE MARKET
Airport Avenue off Bundy
Santa Monica
323-933-2511
www.wertzbrothers.com
Fourth Sunday of each month

connecticut

ANTIQUES IN A COW PASTURE
92 Canaan Road
Salisbury
845-876-0616
Early September

FARMINGTON ANTIQUES WEEKEND
Town Farm Road
Farmington
317-598-0012
www.farmington antiques.com
Two weekends each year

florida

WEST PALM BEACH ANTIQUE AND COLLECTIBLE SHOW
South Florida Fairgrounds
West Palm Beach
561-640-3433
www.dmgantiquesshow.com
First weekend of each month

georgia

HISTORIC LAKEWOOD ANTIQUES MARKET
Lakewood Fairgrounds
Atlanta
404-622-4488
www.lakewoodantiques.com
Every second weekend of each month

PRIDE OF DIXIE
North Atlanta Trade Center
Atlanta
770-279-9899
www.northatlantatrade center.com
Fourth weekend of each month

SCOTT ANTIQUE MARKET
3850 Jonesboro Road
Atlanta
740-569-2800
www.scottantiquemarket.com
Second weekend of each month

massachusetts

BRIMFIELD ANTIQUE SHOWS WEEK
Brimfield
413-283-2418
www.brimfieldshow.com
Three times a year, in May, July, and September

new jersey

LAMBERTVILLE ANTIQUES MARKET
1864 River Road
Lambertville
609-397-0456
Wednesday, Saturday, and Sunday

ohio

SPRINGFIELD ANTIQUE SHOW AND FLEA MARKET
Clark County Fairgrounds
Springfield
937-325-0053
www.jenkinsshow.com
Third weekend of each month from April through December

pennsylvania

RENNINGERS ANTIQUE & FARMERS MARKETS
Kutztown
877-385-0104
www.renningers.com
Three times a year in April, June, and September

texas

ROUND TOP ANTIQUES FAIR
Round Top
281-493-5501
www.roundtopantiques fair.com
First weekend in April and October

SAN ANTONIO FLEA MARKET
12280 Highway 16 South
San Antonio
210-624-2666
Weekends

PARIS

Paris is all about style, good taste, and glamour. Everything from a simple pastry to a pair of designer shoes speaks of a city that values aesthetics above all else. It's difficult to appreciate its visual splendor adequately, because almost every corner, every shop window, every antiques stall has something to "ooh" and "aah" about. There is always too much to see and too much to do, a surfeit of wonderful antiques, food, museums, and fashion in an overflowing elegant box tied with beautiful silk ribbons containing everything I adore. All those who love Paris have their own favorite places, so here are mine, which I hope you will enjoy as you explore this magical city.

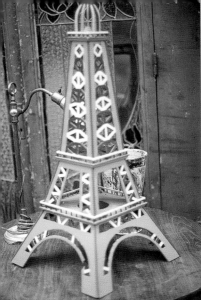

Antiques Shops

Paris has some of the best antiques shopping in the world. In the heart of the ritzy seventh arrondissement on the Left Bank are 120 fashionable antiques shops and art galleries with some of the best decorative art around. Called "Carré Rive Gauche," the shops are bounded on two sides by the quai Voltaire and the rue de l'Université and by the rue du Bac to the rue des Saint-Pères on the other two, making a square area of several blocks. You can wander for hours from one shop to another and then stroll up the boulevard Saint-Germain and have a drink at Café de Flore or lunch at Brasserie Balzar. For a little map of the area and a list of all the dealers, access www.carrerivegauche.com. Here are some favorites.

ANTIQUITÉS
25, rue de Beaune
011-33-01-40-15-99-20

CATHERINE ARIGONI
14, rue de Beaune
011-33-01-42-60-50-99

AURÉLIE ANTIQUAIRES
12, rue de l'Echaudé
011-33-01-46-33-59-41

LE CABINET DE
CURIOSITÉS
23, rue de Beaune
011-33-01-42-61-09-57

MADELEINE CASTAING
21, rue Bonaparte
011-33-01-43-54-91-71

LAURENT CHALVIGNAC
29, rue de Lille
011-33-01-42-61-60-07

TIANY CHAMBARD
32, rue Jacob
011-33-01-43-29-73-15

COMOGLIO PARIS
22, rue Jacob
011-33-01-43-54-65-86

PHILIPPE DELPIERRE
3, rue du Bac
011-33-01-47-03-32-25

DEYROLLE
46, rue du Bac
011-33-01-42-22-30-07

FRÉMONTIER
ANTIQUAIRES
5, quai Voltaire
011-33-01-42-61-64-90

FRANÇOIS FONTÈS
33, quai Voltaire
011-33-01-42-61-81-34

GALERIE DE BEAUNE
7, rue de Beaune
011-33-01-42-86-05-72

GALERIE DUVEAU-SAGE
42, rue de Verneuil
011-33-01-42-61-83-56

GALERIE HUMEURS
3, rue de l'Université
011-33-01-42-86-89-11

GALERIE KATIA
7, rue du Bac
011-33-01-42-61-13-15

FRANÇOIS HAYEM
13, rue du Bac
011-33-01-42-61-25-60

CHRISTINE LENGLET
12, rue de Beaune
011-33-01-40-20-02-28

SYLVAIN LÉVY-ALBAN
14, rue de Beaune
011-33-01-42-61-25-42

LE RIDEAU DE PARIS
32, rue du Bac
011-33-01-42-61-18-56

MARIE-CHRISTINE DE
LA ROCHEFOUCAULD
16, rue de l'Université
011-33-01-42-86-02-40

WILLIAM VONTHRON
40, rue de Verneuil
011-33-01-42-96-62-32

YVELINE
4, rue Furstenberg
011-33-01-43-26-56-91

Another place where you can see many shops at one time is Le Louvre des Antiquaires, which is located across from the Louvre Museum. Think upscale antiques center, French-style, with 250 shops featuring everything from archaeology to Art Deco under one roof. It's near the Palais Royal, which also has some wonderful antiques shops featuring military medals, lead soldiers, rare books and stamps, and my favorite place for vintage couture clothing and accessories, Didier Ludot. If you want to take a sumptuous break, make reservations to have lunch at the eighteenth-century Le Grand Véfour at the end of the tranquil Palais Royal gardens. The best!

LE LOUVRE DES
ANTIQUAIRES
2, place du Palais Royal
011-33-01-42-97-27-00
Tuesday through Sunday,
11 A.M. to 7 P.M.

DIDIER LUDOT
20, Galerie Montpensier
Jardins du Palais Royal
011-33-01-42-96-06-56

PREVIOUS PAGE, TOP ROW, LEFT TO RIGHT: *Early-morning glimpses of the Marché aux Puces.*

MIDDLE ROW, LEFT TO RIGHT: *Some gastronomic reasons why I love Paris, including tea at the beautiful Hôtel Meurice, pictured in the center.*

BOTTOM ROW, LEFT TO RIGHT: *Le Marché du Livre Ancien, featuring rare and used books and maps, and Les Puces de Vanves are two weekend markets that should not be missed.*

OPPOSITE: *Antiques stacked at Les Puces de Vanves early on Saturday morning.*

The "Triangle Rive Droite" has become a very popular area for antiquing. There are more than eighty very sophisticated and elegant shops and galleries in this area bounded by the rue du Faubourg Saint-Honoré, the avenue Matignon, and the rue de Miromesnil. This is where to go if you are looking for "FFF" (fine French furniture).

DIDIER AARON ET CIE
118, rue du Faubourg
   Saint-Honoré
011-33-01-47-42-47-34

BÉNÉDICTE MARTIN DU
DAFFOY
350, rue du Faubourg
   Saint-Honoré
011-33-01-42-60-67-16

FABRE ET FILES
19, rue Balzac
011-33-01-45-61-17-52

GALERIE JEAN-LOUIS
DANANT
36, avenue de Matignon
011-33-01-42-89-40-15

GALERIE MICHEL MEYER
24, avenue de Matignon
011-33-01-42-66-62-95

KRAEMER ET CIE
43, rue de Monceau
011-33-01-45-63-24-46

J. KUGEL
279, rue du Faubourg
   Saint-Honoré
011-33-01-42-60-86-23

FRANÇOIS LÉAGE
178, rue du Faubourg
   Saint-Honoré
011-33-01-45-63-43-46

CADRES LEBRUN
155, rue du Faubourg
   Saint-Honoré
011-33-01-45-61-14-66

ANDRÉE MACÉ
266, rue du Faubourg
   Saint-Honoré
011-33-01-42-27-43-03

PERRIN ANTIQUAIRE
98, rue du Faubourg
   Saint-Honoré
011-33-01-42-65-01-38

BERNARD STEINITZ
9, rue du Cirque
011-33-01-42-89-40-50

Antiques Shows

BIENNALE DES ANTIQUAIRES
Syndicat National des Antiquaires
011-33-01-44-51-74-74

The Biennale des Antiquaires takes place in Paris every two years, alternating with Florence, Italy. It's a sensational show with the best of the best!

PLACE DE LA BASTILLE
Joel Garcia Organization
42/44 Rue Père Coretin
011-33-01-56-53-93-93

The antiques shows at the Place de la Bastille feature hundreds of dealers with affordable merchandise, under the plane trees along the charming Canal Saint-Martin.

THE EUROPEAN FINE
ARTS FAIR (TEFAF)
(commonly known as the
Maastricht Antiques Fair)

The TEFAF Group
P.O. Box 1035
5200 BA Hertogebosch
The Netherlands

In a small Dutch city every March one of the most important antiques and art fairs in the world takes place. The European Fine Arts Fair (TEFAF) in Maastricht, Holland, on the German-Belgium border, has a superb reputation for gathering together about two hundred of the world's top antiques and art dealers, who come from thirteen countries with a glittering assortment of rare and beautiful objects. The fair is usually divided into six sections: paintings, drawings and prints; twentieth century art; antiques and works of art; classical antiquities and Egyptian works of art; illuminated manuscripts, rare books and maps; and La Haute Joaillerie du Monde (jewelry). The show's remarkably rigorous vetting process, requiring approval by a panel of experts, assures the quality, provenance, and condition of your purchase. It's an amazing show and many of the exhibits are heart-stopping in terms of the quality of merchandise and how sumptuously it is presented. Visiting the two-thousand-year-old medieval town of Maastricht, with its lovely shops, restaurants, and galleries, is a wonderful bonus. It is within easy reach of most European cities and accessible by Thalys, the high-speed train from Paris.

Antiques Markets

LE MARCHÉ AUX PUCES DE SAINT-OUEN

Porte de Clignancourt
Saint-Ouen
Saturday, Sunday, and Monday, 10 A.M. to 6 P.M.
(many dealers are closed on Monday)

At the end of the nineteenth century, the ragpickers of Paris, who gathered everything from broken china and unmatched candlesticks to old clothes and shoes, moved to Saint-Ouen, north of Paris. Le Marché aux Puces de Saint-Ouen has grown to be one of the world's largest antiques markets—often called "the attic of the world"—containing approximately 3,500 dealers (2,500 located in permanent stalls) and selling everything from secondhand goods to elegant French antiques and decorative objects.

I've been going to this flea market for years and can still always find exceptional treasures and the odd bargain.

Saturday and Sunday are the best days to visit. You will need every minute to cover the twelve separate markets here. When you arrive, ignore the sidewalk vendors and head for the main street of the market, the rue des Rosiers, which is connected by some seven miles of passageways that will then take you to all the other markets. (Buy a map of the market when you get there—it will make navigating much easier.)

My favorites are Marché Vernaison, where you'll find small items like silver, weapons, vintage clothes, china, and a wonderful selection of Victorian linens; Marché Paul Bert, shops filled with chic decor, copper pots, chandeliers, and garden furniture; and Marché Serpette, a covered area with magnificent paintings, gilded mirrors, tapestries, everything elegant.

Here are some tips:

- Go by Métro (line 4, Porte d'Orléans–Porte de Clignancourt; then stroll a short distance on the avenue Michelet) or by taxi. If I am planning to buy lots, I reserve a car or a taxi in advance to pick me up in the afternoon. (It is almost impossible to find a taxi at the end of the day.)
- The stalls start opening at a civilized 10 A.M., so don't get there too early.
- There are clean bathrooms and telephones in each market, and restaurants where you can enjoy a fun lunch. Book a table in advance or eat at noon, before the restaurants get crowded. I like Chez Louisette, 136, avenue Michelet, 011-33-01-40-12-10-14; La Chope de Puces, 122, rue des Rosiers, 011-33-01-40-11-02-49; and Le Paul Bert, 20, rue Paul Bert, 011-33-01-40-11-90-28.
- The shippers with offices at the flea market—Camard, Alan Franklin Transport, and Edet—will be happy to send your purchases home.

LES PUCES DE VANVES

Avenue Georges Lafenestre and avenue Marc Sangnier
Saturday and Sunday, 7 A.M. to 2 P.M.

For years I never made the effort to get to this flea market in the fourteenth arrondissement. *Je regrette!* Now I'm making up for lost time. This is one of the most exciting markets in Paris at the moment. Several hundred friendly dealers are set up under chestnut trees on each side of the avenue. The mix is eclectic: Art Deco ceramics, Vuitton luggage, paintings, silver, linens, Bakelite jewelry, vintage clothing, and more. If your quarry is furniture, this is not the place for you. It is, however, the place for everything else! At the corner where both avenues meet is a vendor with the best French fries ever. Start at the beginning of the avenue Marc Sangnier, so you won't miss anything.

LE MARCHÉ DU LIVRE ANCIEN

89-101, rue Brancion at Parc Georges Brassens
Saturday, 9 A.M. to 6 P.M.

Sixty booksellers set up underneath Victorian cast-iron pavilions display a wide choice of books from nonfiction to children's books, as well as maps and engravings. It's the perfect place to browse for rare volumes and first editions, as well as a wide selection of secondhand volumes at reasonable prices. Just across the street at 87, rue Brancion, Max Poilâne, is what I think is the best bakery in Paris where you can buy mouthwatering treats, all utterly sublime.

LE MARCHÉ D'ALIGRE

Place d'Aligre
Saturday and Sunday, 8 A.M. to 12:30 P.M.
Along with twenty to thirty dealers who specialize in bric-a-brac, books, and "what have you" is a wonderful green market where you can buy vegetables, colorful flowers, and wonderful cheeses from beautifully displayed tables. If you have a good eye and don't mind rummaging through cartons, you are bound to find something here.

Auction Houses

Although Sotheby's and Christie's have finally established offices in Paris, I still love attending the auctions at Drouot, which until now has been the only major auction house in France. Two thousand auctions are held each year in its sixteen rooms. For a unique Parisian experience, join the thousands of collectors who spend every free moment here.

DROUOT MONTAIGNE
15, avenue Montaigne
011-33-01-48-00-20-80

DROUOT RICHELIEU
9, rue Drouot
011-33-01-48-00-20-20

Shippers

If you have gone overboard, don't fret. The people listed below will ship all your purchases, including your French country sideboard or anything too heavy to carry home.

ALAN FRANKLIN
TRANSPORT & LOCKSON
Marché aux Puces Saint-Ouen
2, rue Etienne Dolet
011-33-01-40-11-50-00

CAMARD
28, rue Cristino-Garcia
La Plaine Saint-Denis
011-33-01-49-46-10-82

EDET INTERNATIONAL
19, rue de Progrès
Montreuil Cedex
011-33-01-48-59-11-73

HEDLEY'S HUMPERS
6, boulevard de la
Libération
011-33-01-48-13-01-02

Museums

After you have exhausted yourself walking through room after room of the Louvre and taken in all the beautiful treasures, you can focus on all the other wonderful small museums studded like jewels around the city. Most are very special and inexplicably uncrowded.

LA MAISON
EUROPÉENNE DE LA
PHOTOGRAPHIE
5-7, rue de Fourcy
011-33-01-44-78-75-00

MUSÉE DES ARTS
ASIATIQUES-GUIMET
6, place d'Iéna
011-33-01-56-52-53-00

MUSÉE DES ARTS
DÉCORATIFS
107, rue de Rivoli
011-33-01-44-55-57-50

MUSÉE CARNAVALET
23, rue de Sévigné
011-33-01-44-59-58-58

MUSÉE COGNACQ-JAY
8, rue Elzévir
011-33-01-40-27-07-21

MUSÉE DES
CRISTALLERIES DE
BACCARAT
30 bis, rue de Paradis
011-33-01-47-70-64-30

MUSÉE FRAGONARD
39, boulevard des
Capucines
011-33-01-42-60-37-14

MUSÉE JACQUEMART-
ANDRÉ
158, boulevard Haussmann
011-33-01-45-62-11-59

MUSÉE DU JEU DE
PAUME
1, place de la Concorde
011-33-01-42-60-69-69

MUSÉE DU LOUVRE
99, rue de Rivoli
011-33-01-40-20-50-50

MUSÉE DE LA MODE DE
LA VILLE DE PARIS
10, avenue Pierre 1er-de-
Serbie
011-33-01-56-52-86-00

MUSÉE NATIONALE DU
MOYEN-AGE
6, place Paul Painlevé
011-33-01-53-73-78-00

MUSÉE NISSIM DE
CAMONDO
63, rue de Monceau
011-33-01-53-89-06-50

MUSÉE D'ORSAY
1, rue de Bellechasse
011-33-01-40-49-48-14

MUSÉE PICASSO
5, rue de Thorigny
011-33-01-42-71-25-21

MUSÉE RODIN
77, rue de Varenne
011-33-01-44-18-61-10

MUSÉE DE LA VIE
ROMANTIQUE
16, rue Chaptal
011-33-01-48-74-95-38

Organizations

These two worthwhile organizations are involved with preserving France's heritage.

FRIENDS OF VIEILLES
MAISONS FRANÇAISES
180 Maiden Lane
New York, NY 10038
212-734-1651

VERSAILLES FOUNDATION
420 Lexington Avenue
New York, NY 10170
212-983-3436

Hotels

Some of the prettiest hotels I've ever stayed at are in Paris. My current favorites are the Hôtel Meurice, with the friendliest staff and most romantic rooms overlooking the Tuileries Gardens, and the Bristol, with its wonderful rooftop swimming pool and view of the Sacré-Coeur.

HÔTEL LE BRISTOL
112 Rue du Faubourg
   Saint-Honoré
011-33-01-53-43-43-00

HÔTEL MEURICE
228, rue de Rivoli
011-33-01-44-58-10-10

HÔTEL PLAZA-ATHENÉE
25, avenue Montaigne
011-33-01-53-67-66-65

RITZ PARIS
15, place Vendôme
011-33-01-43-16-30-30

Restaurants

The Parisian paradox—with all those fantastic restaurants, how do chic Parisians stay so thin? It was very difficult to make a short list of Paris restaurants, because whether you're stopping for something simple or substantial, the food is delicious almost everywhere. Included are some of my favorite bistros, as well as alluring and enduring classics like Le Grand Véfour. I've also included some patisseries, where you can have afternoon tea or rich hot chocolate with your macaroons.

ALLARD
41, rue Saint-André-des Arts
011-33-01-43-26-48-23

L'AMI LOUIS
32, rue du Verbois
011-33-01-48-87-77-48

AUX CHARPENTIERS
10, rue Mabillon
011-33-01-43-26-30-05

BRASSERIE BALZAR
49, rue des Écoles
011-33-01-43-54-13-67

BUDDHA-BAR
8, rue Boissy d'Anglas
011-33-01-53-05-90-00

CHEZ GEORGES
1, rue du Mail
011-33-01-42-60-07-11

LA FERRONNERIE
18, rue de la Chaise
011-33-01-45-49-22-43

LE GRAND VÉFOUR
17, rue Beaujolais
011-33-01-42-96-56-27

LES OLIVADES
41, avenue de Ségur
011-33-01-47-83-70-09

LE PRÉ CATALAN
Route de Surèsnes
Bois de Boulogne
011-33-01-44-14-41-14

LA RÉGALADE
49, avenue Jean-Moulin
011-33-01-45-45-68-58

TANTE LOUISE
41, rue Boissy d'Anglas
011-33-01-42-65-06-85

afternoon tea

A PRIORI THÉ
35, Galérie Vivienne
011-33-01-42-97-48-75

CAFÉ DE FLORE
172, boulevard Saint-
   Germain
011-33-01-45-48-55-26

DALLOYAU
99, rue du Faubourg
   Saint-Honoré
011-33-01-43-59-18-10

HEDIARD
21, place de la Madeleine
011-33-01-42-66-44-36

HÔTEL MEURICE
228, rue de Rivoli
011-33-01-44-58-10-10

LADURÉE
16, rue Royale
011-33-01-42-60-21-79

MARIAGE FRÈRES
30-32, rue de Bourg-
   Tibourg
011-33-01-42-72-28-11

OPPOSITE: *The Marché aux Puces consists of many smaller markets within, like the Marché Biron pictured here.*

L O N D O N

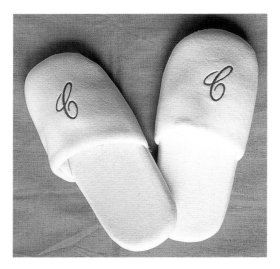

If I ever had to choose just one city to do my antiquing in, it would be London. It's not just the fabulous museums, auction houses, restorers, art galleries, fairs, street markets, and incomparable antiques shops that will forever entice me, but the gentle tradition with which they operate. In all the years I've been collecting, I've always felt that London had time to indulge me, to teach me, to excite me, with a time-honored way of doing business that's hard to find today in the rest of the world.

Any collector worth her salt always leaves London a wiser woman.

COME IN
WE'RE
OPEN
ANTIQUES
OLD
FURNITURE

Antiques Shops

London is still one of the dominant forces in the art and antiques world. For years, connoisseurs have flocked here to buy everything from top-quality antiques and art in Mayfair to wonderful objects in the many small shops that abound.

Most antiques shops and art galleries are clustered together in several neighborhoods: Mayfair and St. James's for the elite in fine art and rare objects, including Bond Street classics like Colnaghi and Partridge Fine Arts; Pimlico Road, where the decorators go for the extraordinary; the King's Road and Kensington Church Street for quirky, treasure-trove shops like the Lacquer Chest.

It's best to do one neighborhood at a time. Each area has some terrific restaurants. For example, at L'Incontro on Pimlico Road, you could end up eating at a table next to David Linley, Princess Margaret's son and furniture maker extraordinaire, who has a shop at 60 Pimlico Road. Serious collectors should look for a British Antiques Dealer Association (BADA) seal in shop windows, which indicates not only excellent stock but also expertise.

mayfair and st. james's

AGNEW'S
43 Old Bond Street
011-44-207-290-9250

ALBEMARLE GALLERY
49 Albemarle Street
011-44-207-499-1616

ARTEMIS FINE ARTS LTD.
15 Duke Street
011-44-207-930-8733

BENTLEY & SKINNER
8 New Bond Street
011-44-207-629-0651

JOHN BLY
27 Bury Street
011-44-207-930-1292

CONNAUGHT BROWN
2 Albemarle Street
011-44-207-408-0362

COLNAGHI
15 Old Bond Street
011-44-207-491-7408

SANDRA CRONAN LTD.
18 Burlington Arcade
011-44-207-491-4851

SIMON C. DICKINSON
58 Jermyn Street
011-44-207-493-0340

ESKENAZI LTD.
10 Clifford Street
011-44-207-493-5464

JOHN ESKENAZI LTD.
15 Old Bond Street
011-44-207-409-3001

SIMON FINCH RARE
BOOKS
53 Maddox Street
011-44-207-499-0974

FINE ART SOCIETY
148 New Bond Street
011-44-207-629-5116

VICTOR FRANSES
GALLERY
57 Jermyn Street
011-44-207-493-6284

FROST & REED
2-4 King Street
011-44-207-839-4645

THOMAS GIBSON FINE
ART
44 Old Bond Street
011-44-207-499-8572

RICHARD GREEN
33 New Bond Street
011-44-207-499-5553
or
147 New Bond Street
011-44-207-493-3939
or
39 Dover Street
011-44-207-499-4738

HANCOCKS & CO.
52-53 Burlington Arcade
011-44-207-493-8904

HOLMES
24 Burlington Arcade
011-44-207-629-8380

DANIEL KATZ
13 Old Bond Street
011-44-207-493-0688

MACCONNAL-MASON
GALLERY
14 & 17 Duke Street
011-44-207-839-7693

MALLETT & SON
141 New Bond Street
011-44-207-499-7411

MALLETT AT BOURDON
HOUSE
2 Davies Street
011-44-207-629-2444

MAP WORLD
25 Burlington Arcade
011-44-207-495-5377

MARLBOROUGH FINE
ART
6 Albemarle Street
011-44-207-629-5161

JOHN MARTIN OF
LONDON
38 Albemarle Street
011-44-207-499-1314

MIRABELLE
56 Curzon Street
011-44-237-499-4636

JOHN MITCHELL & SON
160 New Bond Street
011-44-207-493-7567

ROBERT A. NUNN
3 Burlington Arcade
011-44-207-493-0714

RICHARD OGDEN
28-29 Burlington Arcade
011-44-171-493-9136

PAISNEL GALLERY
22 Mason's Yard
Duke Street
011-44-207-930-9293

PARTRIDGE FINE ARTS
144-146 New Bond Street
011-44-207-629-0834

PREVIOUS PAGE, TOP ROW, LEFT TO RIGHT: *Old standbys—some favorite antiques shops in London.*

MIDDLE ROW, LEFT TO RIGHT: *Sir John Soane's Museum and two views of Bermondsey Market.*

BOTTOM ROW, LEFT TO RIGHT: *So many goodies, so little time—a constant refrain.*

W. H. PATTERSON FINE
ARTS
19 Albemarle Street
011-44-207-629-4119

TREVOR PHILIP & SONS
75-A Jermyn Street
011-44-207-930-2954

PULLMAN GALLERY
14 King Street
011-44-207-930-9595

SIMS REED
43-A Duke Street
011-44-207-493-5660

ALISTAIR SAMPSON
ANTIQUES
15 Duke Street
011-44-207-409-1799

SILVER FUND
1 Duke of York Street
011-44-207-839-8935

J. H. BOURDON-SMITH
24 Mason's Yard
Duke Street
011-44-207-839-4714

SPINK
21 King Street
011-44-207-930-5500

SPINK-LEGER PICTURES
13 Old Bond Street
011-44-207-629-3538

JUNE & TONY STONE
5 Burlington Arcade
011-44-207-493-9495

WADDINGTON
GALLERIES
11 Cork Street
011-44-207-851-2200

JOHNSON WALKER
64 Burlington Arcade
011-44-207-629-2615

WARTSKI
14 Grafton Street
011-44-207-493-1141

WATERHOUSE & DODD
26 Cork Street
011-44-207-734-7800

LINDA WRIGGLESWORTH
34 Brook Street
011-44-207-408-0177

pimlico

ADEC
227 Ebury Street
011-44-207-730-5000

ANNO DOMINI
ANTIQUES
66 Pimlico Road
011-44-207-730-5496

ANTIQUUS
90-92 Pimlico Road
011-44-207-730-8681

APPLEY HOARE
ANTIQUES
30 Pimlico Road
011-44-207-730-7070

HILARY BATSTONE
8 Holbein Place
011-44-207-730-5335

BLANCHARD
86-88 Pimlico Road
011-44-207-823-6310

CHRISTOPHER
BUTTERWORTH
71 Pimlico Road
011-44-207-823-4554

CIANCIMINO
99 Pimlico Road
011-44-207-730-9950

CROWTHER OF SYON
LODGE
77 Pimlico Road
011-44-207-730-8668

CHRISTOPHER GIBBS
3 Dove Walk
Pimlico Road
011-44-207-730-8200

NICHOLAS GIFFORD-
MEAD
68 Pimlico Road
011-44-207-730-6233

NICHOLAS GUEDROITZ
24 Pimlico Road
011-44-207-730-3111

ROSS HAMILTON
95 Pimlico Road
011-44-207-730-3015

NICHOLAS HASLAM
12 Holbein Place
011-44-207-730-8623

JOHN HOBBS
107-A Pimlico Road
011-44-207-730-8369

CHRISTOPHER HODSOLL
89-91 Pimlico Road
011-44-207-730-3370

CHRISTOPHER HOWE
93 Pimlico Road
011-44-207-730-7987

HUMPHREY-CARRASCO
43 Pimlico Road
011-44-207-730-9911

JOHN KING
74 Pimlico Road
011-44-207-730-0427

king's road

JOANNA BOOTH
247 King's Road
011-44-207-352-8998

GUINEVERE ANTIQUES
574-580 King's Road
011-44-207-736-2917

CHRISTOPHER JONES
ANTIQUES
618-620 King's Road
011-44-207-731-4655

L & E KRECKOVIC
559 King's Road
011-44-207-736-0753

DAVID MARTIN-TAYLOR
ANTIQUES
558 King's Road
011-44-207-731-4135

RANKIN & CONN
608 King's Road
011-44-207-384-1847

YORK GALLERY
569 King's Road
011-44-207-736-2260

kensington

BERWALD ORIENTAL
ART
101 Kensington Church
Street
011-44-207-229-0800

LUCY B. CAMPBELL
123 Kensington Church
Street
011-44-207-727-2205

COHEN & COHEN
101-B Kensington Church
Street
011-44-207-727-7677

MICHAEL GERMAN
ANTIQUES
38b Kensington Church
Street
011-44-207-937-2771

EILA GRAHAME
ANTIQUES
97c Kensington Church
Street
011-44-171-727-4132

HASLAM & WHITEWAY
105 Kensington Church
Street
011-44-207-229-1145

JONATHAN HORNE
66-C Kensington Church
Street
011-44-207-221-5658

LACQUER CHEST
75 Kensington Church
Street
011-44-207-937-1306

LONDON ANTIQUE
GALLERY
66e Kensington Church
Street
011-44-171-229-2934

E & H MANNERS
66a Kensington Church
Street
011-44-207-229-5516

R & G MCPHERSON
ANTIQUES
40 Kensington Church
Street
011-44-207-937-0812

NEW CENTURY
69 Kensington Church
Street
011-44-207-937-2410

RAFFETY & WALWYN
79 Kensington Church
Street
011-44-207-938-1100

PATRICK SANDBERG
ANTIQUES
150 & 152 Kensington
Church Street
011-44-207-229-0373

Antiques Shows

Almost every Sunday in London, antiques shows take place in various small hotel ballrooms around the city, and they are fun. But I always look forward to the classics, elegant antiques events that occur every year like clockwork, offering fresh merchandise from Britain and all over the world, much of it vetted. Here are the shows you should not miss.

DECORATIVE ANTIQUES AND TEXTILES FAIR

Harvey Management Services Limited
Battersea Park
011-44-207-624-5173
www.decorativefair.com
Decorators head posthaste to this fair when they are in London in April. It's one of my favorites, too, because each of the 135 exhibitors outdoes the others with displays in stylish room settings.

GROSVENOR HOUSE ART AND ANTIQUES FAIR

Le Meridien Grosvenor House
Park Lane
011-44-207-399-8100
www.grosvenor-antiquesfair.co.uk
The Grosvenor House Art and Antiques Fair, always in June, continues to be one of the most impressive antiques events in the world. The best international dealers present the rarest of the rare.

INTERNATIONAL CERAMICS FAIR AND SEMINAR

The Commonwealth Centre
Kensington High Street
011-44-207-734-5491
www.haughton.com
The International Ceramics Fair and Seminar is for those who can't stop collecting porcelain.

LAPADA

535 King's Road
Chelsea
011-44-207-823-3511
www.lapada.co.uk
This fair is held each fall and features one hundred dealer members of the association.

OLYMPIA FINE ARTS AND ANTIQUES FAIRS

Olympia Exhibition Centre
Hammersmith Road
011-44-870-126-1725
www.olympia-antiques.com
This fun fair features affordable antiques and collectibles.

Antiques Markets

When I'm in London I get up bright and early, because the city is filled with fabulous indoor and outdoor antiques markets, where you can find everything from silver tea-caddy spoons to Regency sideboards. The hundreds of dealers at these bustling markets reflect an incredible cross section of mostly British antiques—evocative World War II photographs, Victorian biscuit tins, vintage clothing, Art Deco jewelry. You never know what remnant of the past you are going to pick up in one of these places. Several years ago I found an Hermès "Kelly" bag for a song and that's kept me coming back ever since! For the truly devoted, there's a market open every day of the week.

indoor markets

These stationary markets, similar to multidealer antiques centers, are chockablock with collectibles and antiques. Prices are higher, but the selection justifies the expense.

ALFIE'S ANTIQUE MARKET

13-25 Church Street
011-44-207-723-6066
Tuesday through Saturday, 10 A.M. to 6 P.M.

ANTIQUARIUS

131-145 King's Road
011-44-207-351-5353
Monday through Saturday, 10 A.M. to 5 P.M.

BOND STREET ANTIQUES CENTRE

124 New Bond Street
011-44-207-493-1854
Monday through Saturday, 10 A.M. to 5:30 P.M.

GRAYS ANTIQUE MARKET

58 Davies Street
011-44-207-629-7034
Monday through Friday, 10 A.M. to 6 P.M.

outdoor markets

BERMONDSEY MARKET (NEW CALEDONIAN MARKET)

Bermondsey Street at Bermondsey Square
Friday, 5 A.M. to 2 P.M.

Every Friday morning since about 1949 Bermondsey Market has been the place to be. It was located in the middle of nowhere, on the other side of the Thames opposite the Tower of London. Gentrification has taken over now and the market is smaller—not the discovery it once was. Though the dealers still arrive with their flashlights at 4 A.M., you can safely arrive by eight o'clock and still have a look around. You never know!

CAMDEN PASSAGE ANTIQUES MARKET

Upper Street off Islington High Street
011-44-207-359-0190
Wednesday, 7 A.M. to 2 P.M.; Saturday, 9 A.M. to 2 P.M.

I always enjoy Camden Passage because it is the most civilized of the markets. It's a combination of indoor markets, shops, and arcades all containing antiques. I prefer going on Wednesday, when there are outdoor stalls offering more affordable merchandise. Start at one end and don't stop until you get to the other. Remember to take a breather at one of the nearby chic cafés.

PORTOBELLO ROAD MARKET

Portobello Road
011-44-207-341-5277
Saturday, 9 A.M. to 4 P.M.

Portobello Road has had its ups and downs, but I've always found something that I can't live without there. Start at the top and walk down the long road past arcades, stalls, and barrows filled to the brim with antiques—and more and more reproductions, so beware. Don't miss Westbourne Grove, which bisects Portobello Road and has some of the nicest dealers.

Auction Houses

I always get the newspaper as soon as I arrive so I know what's happening on the London auction scene. Christie's South Kensington is always quirky and fun.

BONHAMS	CHRISTIE'S	CHRISTIE'S SOUTH KENSINGTON	SOTHEBY'S
101 New Bond Street	8 King Street	85 Old Brompton Road	34-35 New Bond Street
011-44-207-629-6602	011-44-207-839-9060	011-44-207-581-7611	011-44-207-293-5000

Shippers

Shipping antiques home from London is easy, because the British have been doing it for centuries. Lockson, for example, will pick up your purchases at many outdoor markets and antiques fairs.

ALAN FRANKLIN
TRANSPORT
26 Black Moor Road
Verwood, Dorset
011-44-1202-826-539

GANDER & WHITE
21 Lillie Road
011-44-207-381-0571

HEDLEY'S HUMPERS
3 St. Leonard's Road
011-44-208-965-8733

LOCKSON
Heath Park Industrial
Estate
Freshwater Road
Chadwell Heath, Essex
011-44-208-597-2889

THE PACKING SHOP
6-12 Ponton Road
011-44-207-498-3255

Museums

Some of the best museums in the world are in this city, which is so rich in history. Be sure not to miss the Victoria & Albert, where you can get lost for days, and the small but special museums like Sir John Soane's Museum and the Wallace Collection, which I love.

APSLEY HOUSE
The Wellington Museum
149 Piccadilly
Hyde Park Corner
011-44-207-499-5676

BRITISH MUSEUM
Great Russell Street
011-44-207-323-8000

COURTAULD INSTITUTE
GALLERY
Somerset House
The Strand
011-44-207-848-2526

FASHION & TEXTILE
MUSEUM
83 Bermondsey Street
011-44-207-403-0222

FREUD MUSEUM
20 Maresfield Gardens
011-44-207-435-2002

NATIONAL GALLERY
Trafalgar Square
011-44-207-747-2885

NATIONAL PORTRAIT
GALLERY
St. Martin's Place
011-44-207-306-0055

QUEEN'S GALLERY
Buckingham Palace
011-44-207-321-2233

ROYAL ACADEMY OF
ARTS
Burlington House
011-44-207-300-8000

SERPENTINE GALLERY
Kensington Gardens
011-44-207-402-6075

SIR JOHN SOANE'S
MUSEUM
13 Lincoln's Inn Fields
011-44-207-405-2107

SOMERSET HOUSE
The Strand
011-44-207-845-4600

TATE BRITAIN
Millbank
011-44-207-887-8008

VICTORIA & ALBERT
MUSEUM
Cromwell Road, South
Kensington
011-44-207-942-2000

WALLACE COLLECTION
Hertford House
Manchester Square
011-44-207-563-9500

outside london

CHISWICK HOUSE
Burlington Lane
011-44-208-995-0508

DULWICH PICTURE
GALLERY
Gallery Road
011-44-208-693-5254

HAM HOUSE
Ham Street
Richmond, Surrey
011-44-208-940-1950

OSTERLEY PARK
Isleworth
Middlesex
011-44-208-560-3918

WINDMILL HILL
Hamstead
011-44-208-435-3471

Organizations

For those of us who are Anglophiles, here is a list of societies of like-minded people. Joining will keep you connected to all the enduring things in Britain that inspire you and do a lot of good, too.

AMERICAN FRIENDS OF
THE ATTINGHAM
SUMMER SCHOOL
285 Central Park West
New York, NY 10024
212-362-0701

AMERICAN FRIENDS OF
THE BRITISH MUSEUM
1 East 53rd Street
New York, NY 10022
212-644-0522

BRITISH AMERICAN
CENTRE
1718 Connecticut Avenue
NW, Suite 410
Washington, DC 20009
202-939-8565

THE ENGLISH SPEAKING
UNION
16 East 69th Street
New York, NY 10021
212-879-6800

THE LANDMARK TRUST
Shottesbrooke, Maidenhead
Berkshire, England
SL6 3SW
011-44-162-882-5925

NATIONAL TRUST OF
GREAT BRITAIN
36 Queen Anne's Gate
London, England
SW1 H9AF
011-44-207-222-9251

THE ROYAL OAK
FOUNDATION
26 Broadway
New York, NY 10004
800-913-6565
www.royal-oak.org

Hotels

I love old movies and I always feel as if I'm in one when I'm staying in London. Claridge's, where I've stayed for years, is an Art Deco splendor. The recently spiffed-up Dorchester, which boasts the glamorous Oliver Messel Suite designed by the extravagant theater designer in 1953, will make you feel like Vivien Leigh and Bette Davis rolled into one.

CLARIDGE'S
Brook Street
011-44-207-629-8860

CONNAUGHT
Carlos Place
011-44-207-499-7070

DORCHESTER
Park Lane
011-44-207-629-8888

MANDARIN ORIENTAL
HYDE PARK
66 Knightsbridge
011-44-207-235-2000

Restaurants

It's never been easier to eat a delicious meal in London. Though foreign flavors in this city are increasingly varied, I still prefer the enduring favorites that never disappoint. Some of the hotel restaurants have been updated, like the Michelin-star Foliage, and classics like the River Café and Clarke's haven't lost their original savor. Since you're in England, don't forget the ritual of afternoon tea, delicious *and* fortifying enough to keep you antiquing for several hours more.

AUBERGINE
11 Park Walk
011-44-207-352-3449

BIBENDUM
Michelin House
81 Fulham Road
011-44-207-581-5817

CLARKE'S
124 Kensington Church
   Street
011-44-207-221-9225

FOLIAGE
Mandarin Oriental Hyde
   Park
66 Knightsbridge
011-44-207-235-2000

GORDON RAMSAY AT
CLARIDGE'S
55 Brook Street
011-44-207-499-0099

THE IVY
1 West Street
011-44-207-836-4751

LA TANTE CLAIRE
Berkeley Hotel
Wilton Place
011-44-207-823-2003

L'INCONTRO
87 Pimlico Road
011-44-207-730-6327

MIN'S
31 Beauchamp Place
011-44-207-589-5080

RIVER CAFÉ
Thames Wharf
Rainville Road
011-44-207-386-4200

SARTORIA
20 Saville Road
011-44-207-534-7000

J SHEEKEY
28-32 St. Martin's Court
011-44-207-240-2565

WHEELER'S
12a Duke of York Street
011-44-207-930-2460

ZAFFERANO
15 Lowndes Street
011-44-207-235-5800

afternoon tea

BROWN'S HOTEL
32 Albemarle Street
011-44-207-493-6020

CLARIDGE'S
The Reading Room
Brook Street
011-44-207-629-8860

FIFTH FLOOR CAFÉ
Harvey Nichols
109-125 Knightsbridge
011-44-207-823-1839

FORTNUM & MASON
181 Piccadilly Circus
St. James's Restaurant
and
Fountain Restaurant
011-44-207-734-8040

THE LANESBOROUGH
1 Lanesborough Place
011-44-207-333-7254

RITZ HOTEL
150 Piccadilly
011-44-207-300-2308

SAVOY HOTEL
The Strand
011-44-207-836-4343

STAFFORD HOTEL
St. James Place
011-44-207-493-0111

DUBLIN

I love Dublin! It's a wonderful place to visit, a walking city inhabited by the most delightfully loquacious people. Once you ask a Dubliner for directions, you wind up having a pleasant fifteen-minute chat—something that would exasperate me at home in New York, but that I welcome here. Ravishing Georgian architecture, beautiful green squares, and statues of famous politicians and beloved writers are just some of the lovely old things that make Dublin so special. From elegant Marsh's Library, built in 1702, to scruffy pubs that reek of the not-so-distant past, this city is a pastiche with excellent antiques shopping thrown in for good measure.

Antiques Shops

The main shopping streets for antiques are Francis Street near Saint Patrick's Cathedral, charming Anne Street, and the Powerscourt Townhouse Centre, with a group of shops that features Irish silver and jewelry. In addition to the antiques I always accumulate when traveling in Ireland, I also end up sending home cartons of books from the many wonderful old bookstores. Be sure to look for the Irish Antique Dealers Association (IADA) logo when shopping for antiques in Ireland.

ANTHONY ANTIQUES
7 Molesworth Street
011-353-1-677-7222

ANTIQUE PRINTS
16 South Anne Street
011-353-1-671-9523

ARCHITECTURAL
CLASSICS
5a South Gloucester Street
011-353-1-677-3557

BEAUFIELD MEWS
ANTIQUES
Woodlands Avenue
Stillorgan
011-353-1-288-0375

LORCAN BRERETON
29 South Anne Street
011-353-1-677-1462

EDWARD BUTLER
ANTIQUES
14 Bachelor's Walk
011-353-1-873-0296

CATHACH BOOKS
10 Duke Street
011-353-1-671-8676

CAXTON PRINTS
63 Patrick Street
011-353-1-453-0060

MICHAEL CONNELL
ANTIQUES
53 Francis Street
011-353-1-473-3898

COURTVILLE ANTIQUES
Powerscourt Townhouse
  Centre
South William Street
011-353-1-679-4042

CRANKS ANTIQUES
Powerscourt Townhouse
  Centre
South William Street
011-353-1-671-4489

H. DANKER
10 South Anne Street
011-353-1-677-4009

DELPHI ANTIQUES
Powerscourt Townhouse
  Centre
South William Street
011-353-1-679-0331

L. & W. DUVALLIER
Powerscourt Townhouse
  Centre
South William Street
011-353-1-260-8960

SEAN EACRETT
ANTIQUES
58 Francis Street
011-353-1-454-9467

JOHN FARRINGTON
ANTIQUES
32 Drury Street
011-353-1-679-1899

FLEURY ANTIQUES
57 Francis Street
011-353-1-473-0878

.FORSYTH'S
89 Francis Street
011-353-1-473-2148

FULLAM ANTIQUES
55 Francis Street
011-353-1-454-0299

PATRICK HOWARD
ANTIQUES
60 Francis Street
011-353-1-473-1126

THE JEWEL CASKET
17 South Anne Street
011-353-1-671-1262

JOHNSTON ANTIQUES
69 Francis Street
011-353-1-473-2384

KEVIN JONES ANTIQUES
65 Francis Street
011-353-1-454-6626

JORGENSEN FINE ART
29 Molesworth Street
011-353-1-661-9758

GERALD KENYON
ANTIQUES
6 Great Strand Street
011-353-1-873-0625

ROXANE MOORHEAD
ANTIQUES
Ivy Lane, 9 Clyde Lane
011-353-1-660-5165

MORRIN ANTIQUES
37 Francis Street
011-353-1-454-0299

NEPTUNE GALLERY
41 South William Street
011-353-1-671-5021

GORDON NICHOL
ANTIQUES
67 Francis Street
011-353-1-454-3322

ODEON
69 Francis Street
011-353-1-473-2384

OMAN ANTIQUE
GALLERIES
20 South William Street
011-353-1-616-8991

O'SULLIVAN ANTIQUES
43 Francis Street
011-353-1-454-1143

ESTHER SEXTON
ANTIQUES
51 Francis Street
011-353-1-473-0909

THE SILVER SHOP
23b Powerscourt
  Townhouse Centre
South William Street
011-353-1-679-4147

GEORGE AND
MICHELINA STACPOOLE
Main Street
Adare, County Limerick
011-353-61-396409

TIMEPIECE
57 Patrick Street
011-353-1-454-0774

UPPER COURT MANOR
ANTIQUES
54 Francis Street
011-353-1-473-0037

J. W. WELDON
18 South Anne Street
011-353-1-677-2742

PREVIOUS PAGE, TOP ROW, LEFT TO RIGHT: *Worth a visit: Newbridge House, Malahide Castle, and Marsh's Library.*

MIDDLE ROW, LEFT TO RIGHT: *Eire specialties: Blue-and-white Dublin pottery and Irish silver.*

BOTTOM ROW, LEFT TO RIGHT: *Old favorites— Caxton Prints, O'Sullivan Antiques, and Johnston Antiques.*

Antiques Shows

IRISH ANTIQUE DEALERS' FAIR

Fair Management
Main Street
Adare, County Limerick
011-353-61-396409
www.iada.ie

The annual Irish Antique Dealers' Fair is three decades old and is usually held at the Royal Dublin Society Hall on the outskirts of the city. Of course, the things to see are the rare Irish pieces, all of which have been vetted. Several years ago, I saw dramatically carved sideboards and library tables by Dublin cabinetmakers, delicate Cork and Waterford cut-glass compotes, beautifully embossed rare books, and lustrous Georgian silver. There was even a grand eighteenth-century portico from a demolished country home.

Auction Houses

These auction houses are great places to find works by Irish painters and all manner of Irish antiques.

JAMES ADAM SALES ROOMS
26 St. Stephen's Green
011-353-1-676-0261
www.jamesadam.ie

O'REILLY'S
126 Francis Street
011-353-1-453-0311
www.oreillysfineart.com

Shippers

Here's how to get that Irish Georgian sideboard home.

OMAN MOVING AND STORAGE
Merchant's Yard
East Wall Road
011-353-1-836-5611
www.oman.ie

Museums

Dublin is a thriving center for culture, and it is home to some of the finest museums and art galleries. If you love period furniture, rare books and manuscripts, paintings, and beautiful objects, you will enjoy the following. For more good information on historic places, call Tourism Ireland at 800-223-6470 or visit their website, www.shamrock.org, or call Dúchas, the Heritage Service of Ireland, at 011-353-1-647-3000, or visit their website, www.heritageireland.ie.

CASINO MARINO
Off Malahide Road
011-353-1-833-1618

CHESTER BEATTY
LIBRARY
Dublin Castle
011-353-1-407-0750
www.cbl.ie

DUBLIN WRITERS
MUSEUM
18/19 Parwell Square
    North
011-353-1-872-2077
www.writersmuseum.com

HUGH LANE GALLERY
Charlemont House
Parnell Square North
011-353-1-874-1903
www.hughlane.ie

THE IRISH
ARCHITECTURAL
ARCHIVE
73 Merrion Square
011-353-1-676-3430
www.iarc.ie

MALAHIDE CASTLE
Malahide, County Dublin
011-353-1-845-2184
www.visitdublin.com

MARSH'S LIBRARY
St. Patrick's Close
011-353-1-454-3511
www.kst.dit.ie/marsh

NATIONAL GALLERY OF
IRELAND
Merrion Square West
011-353-1-661-5133
www.nationalgallery.ie

NATIONAL MUSEUM OF
IRELAND
Kildare Street
Collins Barracks
Benburb Street
011-353-1-677-7444
www.museum.ie

NEWBRIDGE HOUSE
Donabate, County Dublin
011-353-1-843-6534
www.fingal-dublin.com

NEWMAN HOUSE
University College, Dublin
85-86 St. Stephen's Green
011-353-1-475-7255
By appointment

Organizations

The Irish Georgian Society was founded at a time when architectural treasures in Ireland were being thoughtlessly destroyed. Today, when you join you are helping to ensure their future.

IRISH GEORGIAN SOCIETY
74 Merrion Square
Dublin 2 Ireland
011-353-1-676-705

IN THE UNITED STATES:

IRISH GEORGIAN SOCIETY
7 Washington Square North
New York, NY 10003
212-759-7155
www.archeire.com/igs

NATIONAL TRUST FOR IRELAND
Tailors Hall, Back Lane
Dublin 8 Ireland
011-353-1-454-1786
www.antaisce.org

Hotels

I love visiting Dublin so I can stay at the luxurious Merrion hotel. Occupying the last four town houses on Merrion Square, this comfortable hotel, filled with a collection of superb art and antiques, is a perfect base for running around the city. You can return for cozy afternoon tea, stroll in the beautiful flower-filled garden, or swim in their Tethra Spa pool. And since you're in Ireland, play a round of golf at beautiful Carton House Golf Club, just outside Dublin.

CARTON HOUSE GOLF CLUB
Maynooth, Country Kildare
011-353-1-628-6271

THE MERRION HOTEL
Upper Merrion Street
011-353-1-603-0600
www.merrionhotel.com

I've included two elegant country house hotels filled with antiques that are too good to miss if you decide to drive outside of Dublin. Glin Castle, a favorite, is home to the Knight of Glin, Desmond FitzGerald, and his wife, Olda, who write wonderful books on Irish art and gardens.

GLIN CASTLE
Glin, County Limerick
011-353-068-34173 or 800-323-5463
www.glincastle.com

MARLFIELD HOUSE
Gorey, County Wexford
011-353-55-21124
www.marlfieldhouse.com

Restaurants

Until recently one didn't go to Ireland for its food (with the exception of the hearty Irish breakfasts). But there's been a gastronomic revolution and now one should. Dublin boasts some lively restaurants with chic decor, good food, and friendly service.

BEWLEY'S TEA CAFÉ
78 Grafton Street
011-353-1-677-6761

EDEN
Meeting House Square
Temple Bar
011-353-1-670-5372

FITZERS CAFÉ
40 Temple Bar Square
011-353-1-679-0440

GALLAGHER'S BOXTY
HOUSE
20 Temple Bar
011-353-1-677-2762

LA STAMPA
35 Dawson Street
011-353-1-677-8611

LE COQ HARDI
35 Pembroke Road
011-353-1-668-9070

L'ECRIVAIN
109a Lower Baggot Street
011-353-1-661-1919

RESTAURANT PATRICK
GUILBAUD
21 Upper Merrion Street
011-353-1-676-4192

THE TEA ROOM
Clarence Hotel
6-8 Wellington Quay
011-353-1-407-0800

OPPOSITE: *Teatime in the comfortable Drawing Room of the Merrion Hotel, surrounded by art and antiques and overlooking the gardens.*

VENICE, ROME, and FLORENCE

VENICE

As you enter the magnificent Ca' Rezzonico in Venice, there is a marble plaque dedicated to poet Robert Browning, who died there in 1889, loving Italy until the very end. It says: "Open my heart and you will see graved inside of it, Italy." To anyone who can't live without art, antiques, and history in big doses, Italy is the place. Venice, its most seductive city, seems to have resisted time, which is one of the reasons we love it so. After visiting all these years, I still return home with antique keepsakes.

Antiques Shops

Just wander the narrow *calles* and you will encounter many unique little antiques shops. This is the city where glass was invented, so look for precious old Venetian goblets, ornate chandeliers, and sleek modernist designs of the 1950s and 1960s crafted in Murano, which have become so collected lately.

ANTICHITÀ DI BRUNA
MAZZON
Calle de l'Aseo
Cannaregio 1889
011-39-041-711-095

ANTICHITÀ PIETRO
SCARPA
Calle Gambara
Dorsoduro 1023
011-39-041-523-9700

ANTICHITÀ SAN
MAURIZIO
Campo San Maurizio
San Marco 2663
011-39-041-521-2510

ANTICHITÀ ZAGGIA
CLAUDIA
Dorsoduro 1195
011-39-041-522-3159

ANTIQUUS
Calle delle Botteghe
San Marco 3131
011-39-041-520-6395

ATTILIO CODOGNATO
San Marco 1295
011-39-041-522-5042

CENERENTOLA
Calle dei Saoneri
San Polo 2718
011-39-041-523-2006

CLAUDIA CANESTRELLI
Dorsoduro 364A
011-39-041-522-7072

CLAUDIA GIANOLLA
Calle Spezier
San Marco 2766
011-39-041-521-2652

L'ANGOLO DEL PASSATO
Calle del Cappeller
Dorsoduro 3276A
011-39-041-528-7896

LA GONDOLINA
Dorsoduro 860A
011-39-041-277-0371

LORENZO RUBELLI
San Marco 3877
011-39-041-521-6411

LUISA SEMENZATO
San Marco 732
011-39-041-523-1412

LUNA CREAZIONI
San Marco 1850
011-39-041-523-8006

MANÚ
San Marco 1228
011-39-041-522-9294

MANUELA CANESTRELLI
San Barnaba
Dorsoduro 2779
011-39-041-523-0602

MIOTTO
Castello 4945
011-39-041-522-5636

NINFEA
Castello 5228
011-39-041-522-2381

P. E. ZANCOPÈ
San Marco 2674
011-39-041-523-4567

ROSETTIN DIEGO
Dorsoduro 3220
011-39-041-522-4195

STEFANO ZANIN
San Marco 3208
011-39-041-528-5346

SUMITI MAURIZIO
Castello 5274
011-39-041-520-5621

V. TROIS
Campo San Maurizio
San Marco 2666
011-39-041-522-2905

Antiques Markets

ASOLO ANTIQUES MARKET

Piazza del Mercato and surrounding streets
Second weekend of every month except July and August.
Saturday, 3 P.M. until dark; Sunday, 10 A.M. until dark
This is a monthly antiques market just one hour north of Venice in the enchanting Veneto hill town of Asolo that shouldn't be missed. Chic muslin umbrellas set up in the town square and along the winding streets shade tables heaped with antiques. Take a break at the wonderful Caffè Centrale for a refreshing aperitif or stop in at the Villa Cipriani for a drink or dinner in its beautiful garden. Even better, make a day of it and visit some of the most remarkable Palladian villas in the area, many of which are open to the public.

PREVIOUS PAGE, TOP ROW, LEFT TO RIGHT: *Venice: glorious glass, old gardens, and many mirrors.*

MIDDLE ROW, LEFT TO RIGHT: *Rome: Piazza Navona, Via dei Antiques, Hotel de Russie garden.*

BOTTOM ROW, LEFT TO RIGHT: *Florence: A frame specialist, antique outdoor furniture, and small bibelots.*

RIGHT: *Setting up in the Asolo market.*

Museums

In a city of offbeat, specialized museums my most favorite is Ca' Rezzonico, a magnificent palazzo transformed into the most glorious museum dedicated to eighteenth-century life, which also includes an antique apothecary, centuries old, that has recently been restored.

CA' REZZONICO
Fondamenta Pedrocco
Dorsoduro 3136
011–39–041–241–0100

GALLERIE
DELL'ACCADEMIA
Campo della Carita
Dorsoduro 1050
011–39–041–522–2247

MUSEO CORRER
Piazza San Marco
San Marco
011–39–041–522–5625

MUSEO FORTUNY
Campo San Beneto
San Marco 3780
011–39–041–520–0995

MUSEO QUERINI-
STAMPALIA
Campo Santa Maria
Formosa
Castello 5252
011–39–041–271–1411

PALAZZO GRASSI
Campo San Samuele
San Marco 3231
011–39–041–523–1680

PALAZZO MOCENIGO
Salizzada San Stae
Santa Croce 1992
011–39–041–721–798

PEGGY GUGGENHEIM
COLLECTION
Calle San Cristoforo
Dorsoduro 701
011–39–041–520–6288

Organizations

If there is anything worth saving in this world, it is the city of Venice. You can help by joining Save Venice in New York City. It's a organization doing good work and offers a wonderful lecture series.

SAVE VENICE
15 East 74th Street
New York, NY 10021
212-737-3141
www.savevenice.org

WORLD MONUMENTS
FUND
Piazza San Marco
San Marco 63
30124 Venice, Italy
011–39–041–523–761

Hotels

Venice is a city with some very special hotels. Some new favorites of mine are the sumptuous Il Palazzo at the Bauer, impeccably decorated with gorgeous Venetian antiques, and the San Clemente Palace, a restored monastery on its own seventeen-acre private island in the Venetian lagoon.

GRITTI PALACE
Campo Santa Maria del
 Giglio
San Marco 2467
011–39–041–794–611
Fax: 011–39–041–520–0942

HOTEL CIPRIANI
Giudecca 10
011–39–041–520–7744
Fax: 011–39–041–520–3930

IL PALAZZO AT THE
BAUER
San Marco 1413
011–39–041–520–7022
Fax: 011–39–041–520–7557

SAN CLEMENTE PALACE
Isola di San Clemente
San Marco 30124
011–39–041–241–3484
Fax: 011–39–041–296–0083

Restaurants

My husband and I have eaten well in Venice for many years. Be sure to stop in Caffè Florian for a memorable aperitif in the Piazza San Marco—à la Katharine Hepburn. *Buon appetito!*

CIP'S CLUB
Hotel Cipriani
Giudecca 10
011–39–041–520–7744

DA IGNAZIO
Calle dei Saoneri
San Polo 2749
011–39–041–523–4852

HARRY'S BAR
Calle Vallaresso
San Marco 1323
011–39–041–528–5777

LOCANDA CIPRIANI
Isola di Torcello
Torcello 29
011–39–041–730–150

OSTERIA DA FIORE
Calle del Scaleter
San Polo 2202
011–39–041–721–308

TRATTORIA ALLA
MADONNA
Calle della Madonna
San Polo 594
011–39–041–521–0167

VINI DA ARTURO
Calle degli Assassini
San Marco 3656
011–39–041–528–6974

VINO VINO
Calle del Cafetier
San Marco 2007
011–39–041–241–7688

ROME

The esteemed historian John Cornforth once wrote that Mario Praz's books were essential for survival on a desert island. Now that Praz's Roman apartment, the Palazzo Primoli, is a museum, we have yet another good reason to visit this ancient city . . . not that we need one. Its remarkable museums, churches, monuments, and historic streets reflect the grandeur of a rich, illustrious past. After all, the the city is more than 2,700 years old. Buying antiques is fun here because the Italians love to trade.

Antiques Shops

The antiques emporiums in Rome feature everything from rare Renaissance bronzes to affordable bric-a-brac. Most are located on the Via del Babuino and its side streets, from the Spanish Steps to the Palazzo del Popolo, where the newly restored seventeenth-century gardens of the Hotel de Russie are located. The Via dei Coronari also is lined with shops from the Piazza Navona.

ALBERTO DI CASTRO
Via del Babuino 71
011-39-06-699-40267

ANTICHITÀ
ARCHEOLOGIA
Largo della Fontanella di
    Borghese 76
011-39-06-687-6656

CARLO LAMPRONTI
Via del Babuino 69
011-39-06-678-2947

GIULIANA DI CAVE
Via dei Pastini 23
011-39-06-678-0297

LUISA RUBELLI & C.
Via del Babuino 86
011-39-06-320-7664

MARBLE DESIGN
Via del Babuino 25
011-39-06-361-0963

NARCISO RODRIGUEZ
Via Borgognona 4
011-39-06-699-23381

NAVONA ANTIQUARIATO
Piazza Navona 52
011-39-06-687-9639

UMBERTO VISCA
Via Vittoria 42
011-39-06-679-4859

VERDINI C. ANTICHITÀ
Via Zanardelli 22
011-39-06-686-1850

Antiques Markets

MERCATO DI PORTA PORTESE

Near Ponte Sublico, Trastevere
Sunday, 6 A.M. to 2 P.M.
Although there are many bustling outdoor markets (the Campo dei Fiori, for example) in Rome, most of them are filled with flowers, fresh produce, clothes, and household goods—not antiques. The Porta Portese, Rome's outdoor flea market, can be really disappointing in terms of collectibles. If you get the urge, go around nine A.M. and leave your valuables behind because of pickpockets!

MERCATO DELLE STAMPE

Largo Fontanella di Borghese
Saturday, 9 A.M. to 5 P.M.
This edited little market, off the Via Condotti, specializes in engravings, prints, maps, and books.

AREZZO MARKET

Piazza Vasari to Piazza San Francesco
First Saturday and Sunday of each month
Most Romans go to the big market in Arezzo for their antiques fix—it's only an easy one-and-a-half-hour train ride away. The market starts almost at the station and winds its way through town.

Museums

I've already mentioned the Mario Praz Museum, just one of the extraordinary museums in Rome. Visit the twelve-museum Vatican complex, which contains magnificent treasures, and make a reservation several days in advance to enjoy the architectural beauty of the Vatican Gardens.

CERAMIC MUSEUM
PALAZZO BRUGIOTTI
Via Cavour 67
011-39-06-346-136

GALLERIA BORGHESE
Piazza Scipione Borghese 5
011-39-06-841-7645
Reservations suggested; call
011-39-06-328-101

GALLERIA DORIA
PAMPHILJ
Piazza del Collegio
Romano 2
011-39-06-679-7323

MARIO PRAZ MUSEUM
Palazzo Primoli
Via Zanardelli 1
011-39-06-686-1089

NATIONAL ETRUSCAN
MUSEUM
Piazzale di Villa Giulia 9
011-39-06-320-1951

NATIONAL GALLERY OF
CLASSICAL ART
Palazzo Corsini
Via della Lungara 10
011-39-06-6880-2323

VATICAN MUSEUMS/
SISTINE CHAPEL
Viale Vaticano
011-39-06-698-84466

VILLA MEDICI
Viale Trinità dei Monti 1
011-39-06-676-1256

Organizations

Make an appointment to visit the American Academy in Rome, which is on the Janiculum Hill. Its Renaissance-style palazzo built by McKim, Mead, and White in 1914 and newly restored gardens are superb. You can become a member and then participate in various activities in Rome and New York.

AMERICAN ACADEMY IN
ROME
Via Angelo Masina 5
Rome 00153
Italy
011-39-06-584-61
Fax: 011-39-06-581-0788
www.aarome.org

IN THE UNITED STATES:

AMERICAN ACADEMY IN
ROME
7 East 60th Street
New York, NY 10022
212-751-7200
Fax: 212-751-7220
www.aarome.org

ITALIAN HISTORIC
HOUSES ASSOCIATION
Largo dei Fiorentini 1
Rome
Italy
011-39-06-683-07426
Fax: 011-39-06-688-02930

Hotels

Sample "la dolce vita" in the following sumptuous hotels each of which has its own lush garden. La Poste Vecchia, a favorite, is just outside Rome.

HASSLER
Piazza Trinità dei Monti 6
011-39-06-699-340
Fax: 011-39-06-678-9991

HOTEL DE RUSSIE
Via del Babuino 9
011-39-06-328-881
Fax: 011-39-06-328-88888

LA POSTA VECCHIA
Palo Laziale, Ladispoli
011-39-06-994-9501
Fax: 011-39-06-994-9507

Restaurants

When in Rome, start the day with a cornetto and cappuccino at the historic Antico Caffè Greco.

AGATA E ROMEO
Via Carlo Alberto 45
011-39-06-446-6115

ANTICO CAFFÈ GRECO
Via Condotti 86
011-39-06-679-1700

DAL BOLOGNESE
Piazza del Popolo 1
011-39-06-361-1426

IL CONVIVIO
Via dell'Orso 44
011-39-06-686-9432

LA CAMPANA
Vicolo della Campana 18
011-39-06-686-7820

LA ROSETTA
Via della Rosetta 8
011-39-06-686-1002

PIERLUIGI
Piazza de' Ricci 144
011-39-06-686-8717

PIPERNO
Via Monte de' Cenci 9
011-39-06-688-06629

FLORENCE

Florence has been a special place for me since I worked there when I was just starting out in the corporate world. Things have changed. I no longer have a Mary Quant haircut or wear a miniskirt. Every Italian now has a cell phone, and the lira has succumbed to the pallid euro. Yet it's still possible to visit the secret Porcelain Museum (Museo della Porcellana) in an old palazzo at the top of the Boboli Gardens and gaze down at a countryside view that has not changed in centuries. This is the Italy we all love.

Antiques Shops

There are some magnificent antiques shops in Florence, clustered together in two areas: on or near the Via dei Fossi and on the opposite side of the River Arno, on and off the Via Maggio.

ALLESANDRO CAMPOLMI
Via Maggio 5
011–39–055–295–367

ANTICHITÀ
Via dei Fossi 7
011–39–055–217–092

ANTICO SETIFICIO
FIORENTINO
Via Bartolini 4
011–39–055–213–861

ANTONELLA PRATESI
Via dei Fossi 7
011–39–055–287–683

ANTONIO ESPOSITO
Via Maggio 82
011–39–055–289–173

ATELIER MELISSA
GENTILE
Via Fossi 7
011–39–055–264–432

BARTOLOZZI E MAIOLI
Via Maggio 13
011–39–055–282–675

BOTTEGA SAN FELICE
Via Maggio 39
011–39–055–215–479

BUCCELLATI
Via Tornabuoni 71
011–39–055–239–6579

DINOLEVI
Via Maggio 53
011–39–055–212–815

GALLORI-TURCHI
Via Maggio 14
011–39–055–282–279

GIAMPAOLO FIORETTO
Borgognissanti 43
011–39–055–214–927

GUIDO BARTOLOZZI
Via Maggio 18
011–39–055–215–602

HALL INTERNATIONAL
Borgognissanti 58
011–39–055–287–428

ISABELLA M.
BRANCOLINI
Via Maggio 7
011–39–055–210–531

LEONARDO CAPPELLINI
Via del Presto di San
Martino 20
011–39–055–282–935

LIBRI D'ARTE
Borgo S. Jacopo 68
011–39–055–239–6696

LUCIA CASELLI
Via Maggio 17
011–39–055–239–6422

MANLIO AGLIOZZO
Via Maggio 24
011–39–055–292–398

MASINI
Sdrucciolo dei Pitti 21
011–39–055–293–093

MASSIMO VEZZOSI
Via dei Fossi 29
011–39–055–294–549

MIRELLA PISELLI
Via Maggio 23
011–39–055–239–8029

PAMPALONI
Borgo Santi Apostoli 47
011–39–055–289–094

PITTI ANTIQUES
Piazza Pitti 15
011–39–055–295–295

SANDRO MORELLI
Via Maggio 51
011–39–055–282–789

SETTEPASSI-FARAONE
Via Tornabuoni 25
011–39–055–215–506

U. GHERARDI
Ponte Vecchio 5
011–39–055–211–809

Antiques Shows

THE BIENNALE

Mostra Mercato Internazionale dell'Antiquariato
Palazzo Corsini
Via de Parione 11
011–39–055–282–283
www.biennale@mostraantiquariato.it

There are many antiques shows in Florence throughout the year. I always ask the concierge in my hotel what's doing during my stay. The Biennale, however, is the most prestigious show and occurs in Italy, alternating with Paris, every two years at the end of September.

Antiques Markets

AREZZO MARKET

Piazza Vasari to Piazza San Francesco

First Saturday and Sunday of each month

This remarkable antiques market, an easy one-hour train ride outside of Florence, starts almost at the station and winds its way through town, so you can forage for wonderful treasures at each dealer and see a part of Arezzo as well.

If you are in Florence over a weekend, it's fun to browse in both of these little street markets.

MARKET OF SANTO SPIRITO

Piazza Santo Spirito

Last Sunday of each month

PIAZZA DEI CIOMPI FLEA MARKET

Piazza dei Ciompi

First Sunday of each month

Museums

Florence was the birthplace of the Renaissance, so its museums are filled with incredible architectural treasures, sculptures, and paintings.

BARGELLO MUSEUM
Via del Proconsolo 4
011-39-055-238-8606

BIBLIOTECA MEDICEA
LAURENZIANA
Piazza San Lorenzo 9
011-39-055-210-760

BRANCACCI CHAPEL
Piazza del Carmine
011-39-055-238-2195

COSTUME GALLERY
Pitti Palace
Piazza Pitti
011-39-055-238-8713

FERRAGMO MUSEUM
Via dei Tornabuoni 2
011-39-055-336-0456
By appointment only

GALLERIA
DELL'ACCADEMIA
Via Ricasoli 60
011-39-055-2388-609

MUSEO DELLE
PORCELLANA
Boboli Gardens
Pitti Palace
011-39-055-238-8605

MUSEO DELL'OPERA DEL
DUOMO
Piazza del Duomo 9
011-39-055-230-2885

PITTI PALACE
Palazzo Pitti
011-39-055-238-8615

UFFIZI GALLERY
Loggiato degli Uffizi 6
011-39-055-238-85

VASARI CORRIDOR
Uffizi Gallery
011-39-055-283-044

VILLA I TATTI
Via di Vincigliata 26
011-39-055-603-251
By appointment

Hotels

You won't go wrong staying at either of the pretty hotels listed here; each has beautiful views.

BEACCI TORNABUONI
Via Tornabuoni 3
011-39-055-212-645
Fax: 011-39-055-283-594

GRAND HOTEL
Piazza Ognissanti 1
011-39-055-288-781
Fax: 011-39-055-217-400

HOTEL SAVOY
Piazza della Repubblica, 7
011-39-055-27351
Fax: 011-39-055-273-588

VILLA CORA
Viale Machiavelli, 18
011-39-055-229-8451
Fax: 011-39-055-229-096

Restaurants

I've enjoyed these places since my first visit to Florence many years ago and I keep going back. Be sure to sample the Florentine specialties such as *ribolitta* (Tuscan soup) and the rich gelati.

BUCA DELL'ORAFO
Volta dei Girolami 29
011-39-055-213-619

CAFFÈ RICCHI
Piazza Santo Spirito 8
011-39-055-215-864

CAMMILLO
Borgo San Jacopo 57
011-39-055-212-427

CIBRÈO
Via Andrea del Verrocchio
118
011-39-055-234-1100

ENOTECA PINCHIORRI
Via Ghibellina 87
011-39-055-242-7757

I DUE G
Via B. Cennini 6
011-39-055-218-623

RIVOIRE
Piazza della Signoria 5
011-39-055-214-41

TRATTORIA ANTICO
FATTORE
Via Lambertesca 1
011-39-055-238-1215

HELSINKI, HONG KONG, and VIENNA

HELSINKI

Surrounded by water on three sides, the capital of Finland is a stylish city with wide tree-lined streets. Known for its trendsetting design in home furnishings, jewelry, and clothes, it should not be dismissed by the antiques lover. Its Modernist architecture is superb, but its nineteenth-century pale pastel buildings remind us that the country was a grand duchy in the Russian empire until 1917. You can speak English and be understood almost everywhere—especially in the markets and antiques shops.

Antiques Shops

I found a surprising amount of good antiques shops in Helsinki. Most of them are located in two major areas, around Mariankatu Street near Senate Square and in the Kruununhaka District. In addition to wonderful Finnish and Scandinavian antiques like Gustavian painted furniture, folk art, and brass, you'll find Russian treasures like silver tableware and precious porcelain. My big discovery was an Italian nineteenth-century micro-mosaic brooch of the Roman Coliseum found in a tiny shop.

AERO
Annankatu 11
011-358-09-680-2185

ALBERTINA
Mariankatu 24
011-358-09-135-2855

ANTIIKKILIIKE SALIN PUOLI
Mariankatu 14
011-358-09-626-436

ANTIK OSKAR
Rauhankatu 7
011-358-09-135-7410

ATLAS ANTIQUES OY
Rauhankatu 8
011-358-09-628-186

BOUTIQUE SANDRA
Fredrikinkatu 37
011-358-09-671-590

COUNTRY ROSE OY
Mariankatu 14
011-358-09-656-674

DESSEIN OY
Aleksanterinkatu 28
011-358-09-627-745

GALERIE DONNER
Merikatu 1
011-358-09-664-547

GARDEN SHAKERS
Mariankatu 17
011-358-09-278-1162

HAGELSTAMIN KIRJAKAUPPA
Fredrikinkatu 35
011-358-09-649-291

KAUNIS
Mariankatu 17
011-358-040-588-9998

NASTA
Liisankatu 15
011-358-040-702-7973

OLD JOY
Mariankatu 19
011-358-09-135-4675

OLD TIMES
Annankatu 12
011-358-09-604-606

VIA GALLERIA
Uudenmaankatu
011-358-09-612-1871

Antiques Markets

Visit Helsinki in summer and the land of the midnight sun (fifteen hours of sunlight daily) offers untold bleary-eyed excursions to one open-air market after another! The best known in Market Square offers everything from wild berries and luscious flowers to bargain-priced beautiful Scandinavian crafts. At the flea markets, you can find everything from vintage clothes to antique Russian silver pieces and old books.

HIETALAHTI FLEA MARKET

Bulevardi
Open all year, Monday to Saturday, 8 A.M. to 2 P.M.; Sunday, May 7 to October 1, 10 A.M. to 4 P.M.

VR FLEA MARKET

Behind the main post office in the old rail yard
Saturday and Sunday, 10 A.M. to 4 P.M.; Wednesday, 4 P.M. to 8 P.M.

PREVIOUS PAGE, TOP ROW, LEFT TO RIGHT: *Helsinki: Unexpected treasures await in the various shops.*

MIDDLE ROW, LEFT TO RIGHT: *Hong Kong: On the prowl for antiques on Cat Street.*

BOTTOM ROW, LEFT TO RIGHT: *Vienna: The elegant Museum District, and shopping in the city center.*

OPPOSITE: *Two views of the Hietalahti Flea Market on Saturday morning. Wooden ice skates, left, and busts of Lenin and friends from an earlier era.*

Auction Houses

HAGELSTAM
Bulevardi 9
011-358-09-687-7990
Hagelstam is on the way to the Hietalahti Flea Market, so you can visit both on the same day.

Museums

Helsinki contains some very unique museums. The cutting-edge examples, like the new Kiasma Museum of Contemporary Art, are too high-tech for me. I still prefer those filled with glorious objects and furniture that highlight Finnish history and decorative arts.

ARABIA MUSEUM
Hämeentie 135
011-358-01-02-395-353

ATENEUM
Kaivokatu/Brunnsgatan 2
011-358-09-1733-61

DIDRICHSEN ART
MUSEUM
Kuuailahdenkuja 1
011-358-09-489-055

KIASMA
Mannerheiminaukio 2
011-358-09-1733-6500

KIRPILÄ ART
COLLECTION
Pohjoinen Hesperiankatu 7
011-358-09-494-436

MILITARY MUSEUM
Maurinkatu 1
011-358-09-1812-6381

MUSEUM OF ART AND
DESIGN
Korkeavuorenkatu 23
011-358-09-622-0540

MUSEM OF FINNISH
ARCHITECTURE
Kasarmikatu 24
011-358-09-856-75100

PHOTOGRAPHIC
MUSEUM OF FINLAND
Tallberginkatu 1F
011-358-09-6866-3621

REITZ FOUNDATION
Apollonkatu 23
011-358-09-442-501

SINEBRYCHOFF MUSEUM
OF FOREIGN ART
Bulevardi 40
011-358-09-1733-6460

Hotels

Opened in 1887 and designed in the Biedermeier style, the five-star Hotel Kamp is one of my favorites. Its central location in this walking city is perfect for exploring the wonderful shops on the Esplanadi, including colorful Marimekko and the famous Stockmann Department Store.

HOTEL KAMP
Pohjoisesplanadi 29
011-358-09-576-111
Fax: 011-358-09-576-1122

Restaurants

Helsinki has something for everyone's taste, claiming to serve forty different types of cuisine, including the traditional restaurants serving Russian or Finnish food. Many are still located in the beautiful old buildings where they originated. Here's a little bit of everything.

CAFE ESPLANAD
Pohjoisesplanadi 37
011-358-09-665-496

CAFÉ STRINDBERG
Pohjoisesplanadi 33
011-358-09-681-2030

CHEZ DOMINIQUE
Ludviginkatu 3-5
011-358-09-612-7393

GEORGE
Kalevankatu 17
011-358-09-647-110

HAVIS AMANDA
Pohjoisesplanadi 17
011-358-09-666-882

KANAVARANTA
Kanavaranta 3E-F
011-358-09-622-2633

KAPPELI
Eteläesplanadi 10
011-358-09-179-242

LYON
Mannerheimintie 56
011-358-09-408-131

PALACE
Eteläranta 10
011-358-09-134-561

SALI RAVINTOLA
TEATTERI
Pohjoisespa 2
011-358-09-658-113-10

SUNDMANS
Eteläranta 16
011-358-09-622-6410

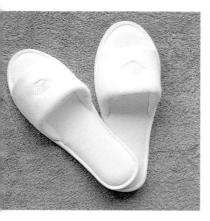

HONG KONG

It was always my dream to visit Hong Kong, and I was not disappointed when I did. It has something for everyone—tall, sophisticated skyscrapers and tiny winding passageways where one can find everything from fresh fruit to expensive jewelry. It's a city of contrasts, constantly in motion, and a must-visit for anyone who loves to shop, especially for antiques.

Antiques Shops

The minute I arrived in Hong Kong, I hit the streets. Shanghai Tang was just around the corner from my hotel, along with shops offering Chinese folk crafts, handmade papers, luxurious pearls, and bargain designer knock-offs. The most fun, however, was the fabulous antiquing. Hollywood Road (named after the English country estate of Sir John Davis, an eighteenth-century governor of Hong Kong) is an antique lover's paradise. Antiques and junk shops line both sides of the road for about a mile. The Man Mo Temple, overflowing with fragrant sandalwood, is a must-see. Nearby Cat Street is filled with more antiques shops.

You may have trouble telling the antiques from the copies, since some of the fakes go back five hundred years! The laws on exporting antiques are always changing, so go to a reputable dealer who gives you the proper papers with the item, verifying its age and all the other pertinent details.

ARCH ANGEL ANTIQUES
53-55 Hollywood Road
011-852-2851-6828

ASIART CORNER
8 Lok Ku Road
011-852-2543-1860

CHINA ART
15 Hollywood Road
011-852-2840-0816

TERESA COLEMAN FINE
ARTS LTD.
79 Wyndham Street
011-852-2526-2450

DRAGON CULTURE
231 Hollywood Road
011-852-2545-8098

HONEYCHURCH
ANTIQUES LTD.
29 Hollywood Road
011-852-2543-2433

MOON GARDEN TEA
HOUSE
149 Hollywood Road
011-852-2541-3887

MOUNTAIN FOLKCRAFT
12 Wo On Lane
011-852-523-2817

PHINNS
24 Upper Lascar Row
011-852-2345-3718

TREASURE COURT
168C Hollywood Road
011-852-2540-1157

TRUE ARTS & CURIOS
89-91 Hollywood Road
011-852-2559-1485

WAH CHEONG CO.
3 Upper Lascar Row
011-852-544-607

WILLOW GALLERY LTD.
159-163 Hollywood Road
011-852-2544-0996

YEE HING LOONG
151 Hollywood Road
011-852-2851-2338

YUE CHUNG HIN
82 Hollywood Road
011-852-2546-9786

YUE PO CHAI ANTIQUE CO.
132-136 Hollywood Road
011-852-2540-4374

macau

Macau is just a short ferry trip from Hong Kong and worth the stop.

ASIA ARTIFACTS
25 Rua dos Negociantes
Coloane Island
011-853-881-022

CHUNG YU TRADING
COMPANY
36 Rua da Tercene
011-853-921-309

HANG MEI
5A Rua de Santo Antonio
011-853-956-585

HONG LEI HONG
60 Rua de Santo Paulo
011-853-368-984

IONG KIN KEONG
38B Ruade 5 Paulo
011-853-368-990

MIN CHAI
34C Rua de Santo Paulo
011-853-362-392

ORIGINS
27 Rua de Santo Paulo
011-853-369-171

TIN LONG
2 Rua de Santo Antonio
011-853-358-608

TONG YUK TONG
2 Rua de Santo Antonio
011-853-365-929

Antiques Markets

I love, love, love outdoor markets and Hong Kong has one for every taste. There is a flower market, a ladies' market, a fish market, a designer knock-off market, and even a bird market. Some of the best ones are the antiques and flea markets that I have listed here.

CAT STREET MARKET
Cat Street, just below Hollywood Road
Daily, with more stalls on the weekends

JADE MARKET
Kansu Street
Yau Ma Tei
Daily, 10 A.M. to 2 P.M.

TEMPLE STREET NIGHT MARKET
Jordan Road
Daily, after 6 P.M.

UPPER LASCAR ROW MARKET
Off Queen's Road West
Daily, 11 A.M. to 6 P.M.

WESTERN MARKET
New Market Street
Daily, 10 A.M. to 7 P.M.

Museums

You may find you are so busy dashing about the city that there is barely time to visit the many museums. Here, nevertheless, is a short list of some that you shouldn't miss. If you only have time for one, go to the Museum of Tea Ware, which is in one of the oldest, most elegant buildings in Hong Kong.

HONG KONG MUSEUM
OF ART
Hong Kong Cultural
   Centre Complex
10 Salisbury Road
Tsim Sha Tsui, Kowloon
011-852-2721-0116

LEI CHENG UK HAN
TOMB MUSEUM
41 Tonkin Street
Sham Shui Po, Kowloon
011-852-2386-2863

MUSEUM OF TEA WARE
Flagstaff House
Hong Kong Park
10 Cotton Tree Drive
   Central
011-852-2869-0690

TSUI MUSEUM OF ART
4/F Henley Building
5 Queen's Road
   Central
011-852-2868-2688

Hotels

A trip to Hong Kong is always special if you stay at the scrumptious Mandarin Oriental Hotel. It is decorated with a noteworthy collection of Chinese antiques, rare textiles, carved gilt screens, and statuary displayed in the guest rooms and public spaces—it also has a wonderful spa.

MANDARIN ORIENTAL
5 Connaught Road
Central
011-852-2522-0111
Fax: 011-852-2810-6190

Restaurants

Hong Kong is famous for everything from Asian cuisine (including dim sum, served from breakfast to lunch) to the most sophisticated Pan-American food.

BLUE
43-45 Lyndhurst Terrace
   Central
011-852-2815-4005

THE CAFÉ AT MANDARIN
ORIENTAL
5 Connaught Road
   Central
011-852-2522-0111

THE CHINA CLUB
13/F Old Bank of China
   Building
2A Des Voeux Road
   Central
011-852-2521-8888

LAI CHING HEEN
The Regent Hotel
18 Salisbury Road
Kowloon
011-852-2721-1211

LUK YU TEA HOUSE
24-26 Stanley Street
   Central
011-852-2523-5464

SAMMY'S KITCHEN
204-206 Queen's Road
   West
Wanchai
011-852-2548-8400

VONG
Mandarin Oriental
5 Connaught Road
   Central
011-852-2825-4028

YUNG KEE
32-40 Wellington Street
   Central
011-852-2522-1624

vienna

Vienna has always been a new-old city. Its romantic architecture, imperial palaces, churches, and ornate concert halls fill you with nostalgia. On the other hand, it is a spirited city that is always adding something avant-garde, like the new Museums Quartier. I love wandering in this perfect walking city, antiquing, humming Mozart, and stopping (almost too often!) at one of its famous cafés for a meal, a luscious dessert, or rich hot chocolate. Visit the Vienna Tourist Board, www.vienna.info, and www.austrianair.com for more good information.

Antiques Shops

This is the perfect place to buy that Biedermeier desk you've always longed for. The shops are filled with everything from cut-crystal chandeliers to Modernist furniture from great designers such as Josef Hoffman. It's easy to succumb to shopaholic behavior when you remember that you are walking in the steps of Sigmund Freud, Vienna's most famous collector.

C. BÜHLMAYER
Michaelerplatz 6
011-43-1-533-1049

BEL ETAGE
Mahlerstrasse 15
011-43-1-512-2379

REINHOLD HOFSTÄTTER
Bräunerstrasse 12
011-43-1-533-5069

PETER KULCSÁR
Spiegelgasse 19
011-43-1-512-7267

LOBMEYR
Kärntnerstrasse 26
011-43-1-512-0508

EVA PERCO
Spiegelgasse 11
011-43-1-513-5695

JOSEF & ALEXANDER
SCHARL
Plankengasse 7
011-43-1-513-3269

MARCEL WANG
ANTIQUES
Spiegelgasse 25
011-43-1-512-4187

Antiques Markets

It's fun to explore the outdoor flea markets around the city. The Flohmarkt, which is open every Saturday morning, is a favorite. At Easter and Christmastime the city squares are filled with stalls, which offer a little bit of everything.

ANTIQUES MARKET NEAR THE
DANUBE CANAL

Steps from the Salztorbrücke
Saturday afternoons and Sundays, from 10 A.M. to 6 P.M.
Summers only

FLOHMARKT AT NASCHMARKT

400 stalls next to the Naschmarkt
Every Saturday, 8 A.M. to 6 P.M.

THE OLD AM HOF CRAFT AND
ANTIQUES MARKET

Am Hof Platz
Friday and Saturday, 10 A.M. to 6 P.M.

Auction Houses

The Dorotheum, established by Emperor Josef I in 1707 and affectionately called "Tante Dorothee," is the state auction house, which also contains a retail shop selling antiques. Leave time to visit some of the many antiques shops clustered up and down the streets outside.

DOROTHEUM
Dorotheergasse 17
011-43-1-515-600

Museums

If you love to visit museums, there are more than eighty to tempt you. The newest addition is the elegant Liechtenstein Museum, with important Baroque masterpieces. It's hard to choose my favorite—the Silberkammer (Museum of Court Silver and Tableware), featuring thousands of silver and porcelain pieces; the Belvedere, with the sensual paintings of Gustav Klimt; or the MAK, with everything from Renaissance lace to Wiener Werkstätte furniture.

ACADEMY OF FINE ARTS
Schillerplatz 3
011-43-1588-16225

ALBERTINA MUSEUM
Albertinaplatz 1
011-43-1-534-830

AUSTRIAN FOLKLORE
MUSEUM
8, Laudongasse 15-19
011-43-1-406-8905

BELVEDERE
Prinz-Eugen-Strasse 27
011-43-1-795-57134

CLOCK MUSEUM
Schulhof 2
011-43-1-533-2265

GEYMÜLLERSCHLÖSSEL
Khevenhüllerstrasse 12
011-43-1-711-36298

HERMESVILLA
Lainzer Tiergarten 13
011-43-1-804-1324

KUNSTHALLE WIEN
Museum Quarter
Museumsplatz 1
011-43-1-521-8914

LEOPOLD MUSEUM
Museum Quarter
Museumsplatz 1
011-43-1-525-700

LIECHSTENSTEIN
MUSEUM
9, Fürstengasse 1
011-43-1-31957-67

MUSEUM OF APPLIED
ARTS (MAK)
Stubenring 5
011-43-1-711-360

MUSEUM OF FINE ARTS
Maria-Theresien-Platz 1
011-43-1-525-240

MUSEUM OF MILITARY
HISTORY
3, Arsenal, Objekt 18
011-43-1-795-610

SCHÖNBRUNN PALACE
Schönbrunner Schloss-
Strasse 13
011-43-1-811-13239

SILBERKAMMER
(IMPERIAL SILVER
COLLECTION)
Hofburg Palace
Michaelerplatz 1
011-43-1-533-7570

Hotels

The hotels in Vienna have a certain grandeur that is obvious whether you are staying at the Hotel Im Palais Schwarzenberg, a baroque palace in the midst of a landscaped eighteen-acre park or, city center, at the Bristol or Palais Coburg.

BRISTOL
Kärntner Ring 1
011-43-1-515-160
Fax: 011-43-1-516-550

DAS TRIEST
Wiedner Haupstrasse 12
011-43-1-589-180
Fax: 011-43-1-589-1818

HOTEL IM PALAIS
SCHWARZENBERG
Schwarzenbergplatz 9
011-43-1-798-4515
Fax: 011-43-1-798-4714

PALAIS COBURG
Coburg Bastei 4
011-43-1-518-180
Fax: 011-43-1-518-181

Restaurants

Vienna's restaurants are famous for their tasty cuisine and their traditional cafés and pastry shops. Every cup of coffee or hot chocolate arrives *"mit Schlag,"* the richest whipped cream imaginable.

DO & CO
Stephansplatz 12
011-43-1-535-3969

ECKEL
Sieveringer 46
011-43-1-320-3218

FABIO'S
Tuchlauben 6
011-43-1-532-2222

KORSO
Bristol Hotel
Kärntner Ring 1
011-43-1-515-16-546

PLACHUTTA
Wollzeile 38
011-43-1-512-1577

RESTAURANT BAUER
Sonnenfelsgasse 17
011-43-1-512-9871

RESTAURANT IM PALAIS
SCHWARZENBERG
Schwarzenbergplatz 9
011-43-1-798-4515-600

STEIRERECK
Rasumofskygasse 2
011-43-1-713-3168

cafés

CAFÉ CENTRAL
Ecke Herrengasse
011-43-1-533-3764

DEMEL
Kohlmarkt 14
011-43-1-535-1717

DIGLAS
Wollzeile 10
011-43-1-512-8401

LANDTMANN
Dr.-Karl-Lueger-Ring 4
011-43-1-532-0621

OBERLAA
Neuer Markt Stadthaus 16
011-43-1-513-2936

SACHER
Philharmonikerstrasse 4
011-43-1-514-560

SLUKA
Rathausplatz 8
011-43-1-405-7172

Suggested Reading

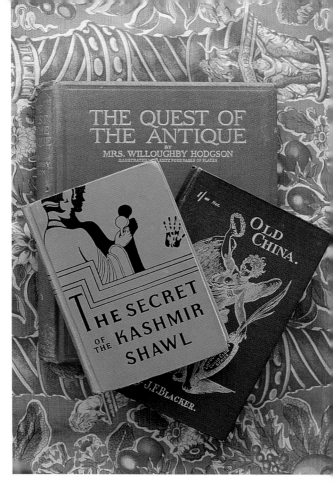

Becker, Robert. Nancy Lancaster: Her Life, Her World, Her Art. *New York: Alfred A. Knopf, 1996.*

Boyer, Marie-France. Paris Style. *London: Weidenfeld & Nicolson, 1989.*

———. Twentieth-Century Decoration. *London: Weidenfeld & Nicolson, 1988.*

Campbell, Nina, and Caroline Seebohm. Elsie de Wolfe, a Decorative Life. *New York: Clarkson N. Potter, 1992.*

Cornforth, John. The Inspiration of the Past. *New York: Viking Press, 1985.*

Crookshank, Anne, and the Knight of Glin. Ireland's Painters *1600–1940. New Haven and London: Yale University Press, 2002.*

Edwards, Ralph. The Shorter Dictionary of English Furniture. *London: Country Life Limited, 1964.*

Fowler, John, and John Cornforth. English Decoration in the Eighteenth Century. *London: Barrie & Jenkins, 1983.*

Girouard, Mark. Life in the English Country House. *New Haven: Yale University Press, 1978.*

Guinness, Desmond, and Jacqueline O'Brien. Great Irish Houses and Castles. *London: Weidenfeld & Nicolson, 1992.*

Havemeyer, Louisine W. Sixteen to Sixty: Memoirs of a Collector. *New York: Ursus Press, 1993.*

Jackson-Stops, Gervase, and James Pipkin. The English Country House: A Grand Tour. *New York: Little, Brown, 1985.*

McFadden, David. L'Art de Vivre: Decorative Arts and Design in France, 1789-1989. *London: Thames and Hudson, 1989.*

Newman, Bruce M. Fantasy Furniture. *New York: Rizzoli, 1989.*

Ohrbach, Barbara M. Antiques At Home. *New York: Clarkson Potter, 1989.*

Praz, Mario. An Illustrated History of Interior Decoration. *New York: Thames and Hudson, 1982.*

Thornton, Peter. Authentic Decor: The Domestic Interior. *New York: Viking Press, 1984.*

Wharton, Edith, and Ogden Codman Jr. The Decoration of Houses. *New York: W.W. Norton, 1997.*

Ypma, Herbert. Irish Georgian. *London: Thames and Hudson, 1998.*

Index

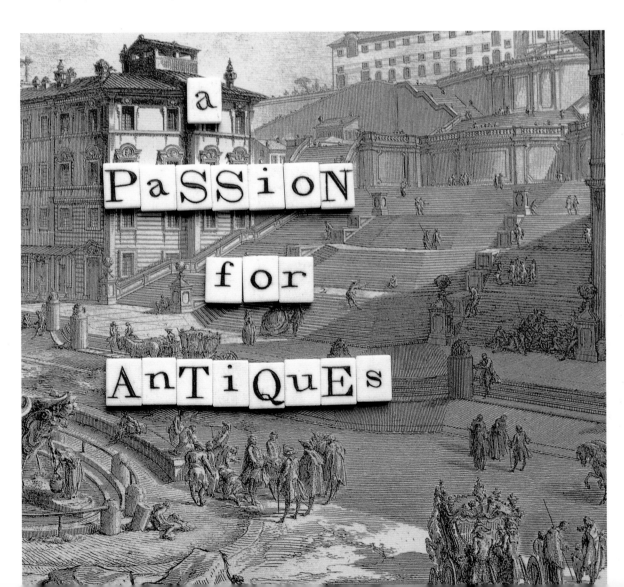

VASES and TRIPODS

delin: ac sculp.